Z979017

Community Learning & Libraries
Cymuned Ddysgu a Llyfrgelloedd

This item should be returned or renewed by the
last date stamped below.

To renew visit:

www.newport.gov.uk/libraries

D1610310

The Tone From the Top

Ian Muir rightly points out that to minimise ethical risk, companies should strengthen their recruitment and assessment processes. The best way to avoid bad apples is to prevent them from joining the organisation in the first place.

James Reed, Chairman, REED

This is an important book in the ongoing discussion of "Tone at the Top". Beginning with a survey of top management makes it stand out. Quotes from those seeking to set the example and embed ethical leadership are telling, as they understand the difficulties of achieving this. These are well illustrated in the variety of case studies in Part II. Whilst Part III may cause readers to stop and think about their own leadership style, and reflect. Anybody reading this engaging book will learn from it, and taking heed will contribute to a better informed, and behaved, leadership in companies, to the benefit of wider society.

Philippa Foster Black CBE, Director, Institute of Business Ethics

The Tone From the Top

How Behaviour Trumps Strategy

IAN MUIR
Keeldeep Associates Ltd, UK

GOWER

Published by
Gower Publishing Limited
Wey Court East
Union Road
Farnham
Surrey, GU9 7PT
England

Gower Publishing Company
110 Cherry Street
Suite 3-1
Burlington, VT 05401-3818
USA

www.gowerpublishing.com

Ian Muir has asserted his right under the Copyright, Designs and Patents Act, 1988, to be identified as the author of this work.

British Library Cataloguing in Publication Data
A catalogue record for this book is available from the British Library.

Library of Congress Control Number: 2014957909

ISBN 9781472454171 (hbk)
ISBN 9781472454188 (ebk – PDF)
ISBN 9781472454195 (ebk – ePUB)

Printed in the United Kingdom by Henry Ling Limited,
at the Dorset Press, Dorchester, DT1 1HD

CONTENTS

LIST OF FIGURES

ACKNOWLEDGEMENTS

This book is dedicated to all leaders wanting to improve their performance and multiply their contribution through their impact on others. It is also dedicated to those who want to see themselves as others see them. Self-awareness in a busy world is a rare gift. My hope is that having read this, more people will take note of how others are influenced by them. For senior people in organisations, much of that influence comes from the tone from the top. The 'tone' is multi-faceted, including policy, process, governance and decisions, but also – and perhaps more importantly, values, behaviour, attitudes and beliefs.

I am very grateful to the following for their help in bringing this book to publication:

All the chairmen who participated in the research
Andrew Campbell and Angela Munro at the Ashridge Strategic Management Centre, Ashridge Business School
Anna Sawyer and everyone at Gallup
The CIPD who worked with me in 2012 to produce a case study 'Consulting employees at Charter International plc' and which is reproduced as Case Study 7
Sue Savage at the CIPD for granting permission to use the case study
Kristina Abbotts, Claire Bell, Sara Hutton, Donna Shanks, Kayleigh Huelin and everyone at Gower
Philippa Foster Black, CBE
The Institute for Business Ethics
James Reed, Chairman at REED plc
Stuart Lindenfield at Reed Global
Nick Robeson at Hemming Robeson
Dr Nigel MacLennan and The Advances in Leadership Conference
Stephen Perkins, Dean Bartlett and London Guildhall faculty of business and law
The Centre for Progressive Leadership
Will Winch and everyone at Mishcon de Reya

Professor Juani Swart at the University of Bath's School of Management
Chris Coffils and everyone at Penna
Ingrid Klinkhammer-Muir for her advice and guidance throughout.

ABOUT THE AUTHOR

Ian Muir is a senior business adviser. He works with leadership teams and individuals to improve organisational performance.

He has worked across five continents, having been an executive committee member at Charter International plc, a director of Cable & Wireless International Group Ltd and a trustee director of a £2.2bn pension fund. He is a graduate of Bath University, a fellow of the Chartered Institute of Personnel & Development and an alumnus of INSEAD. He is also a member of the European Mentoring and Coaching Council and a published author on resilience.

After more than 30 years in corporate life, he now has a portfolio career with three strands: non-executive, independent consulting and working with business schools.

He is a member of the remuneration and appointments committee of one of the UK's medical regulators. His research reports *Board Evaluation* and *The Tone from the Top* were jointly published with Ashridge Business School. All the chairmen in the FTSE350 were sent copies. He has advised the CEOs and executive committees of listed plcs, private equity-owned companies and in the not-for-profit sector. He has undertaken independent board evaluations, delivered executive assessments, advised board executives on HR strategy and coached people aspiring to senior leadership roles.

You can reach him at: *ian.muir@keeldeep.com*

ABOUT ASHRIDGE BUSINESS SCHOOL

Established in 1959, Ashridge is a leading business school for working professionals with an international reputation for executive education and management development. Activities include degree programmes, open enrolment programmes, customised programmes, organisation consulting, academic accreditation services, virtual learning and applied research. It is one of the very few schools worldwide to achieve triple accreditation from AMBA, EQUIS and AACSB; the UK, European and American accreditation bodies.

www.ashridge.org.uk

INTRODUCTION

This book is about leadership, ethical leadership. It is also about how ethical behaviour can enable and sustain organisations. It started life as a research project undertaken by my consulting business, Keeldeep Associates Limited. The research was sponsored by Ashridge Business School. It was driven by a succession of news stories regarding corporate failings and inappropriate conduct by executives. At the time, it seemed that hardly a week went by without another corporate scandal. One media commentator said, 'Truth is stranger than fiction; you could not invent this – the chairman of a major company being prosecuted for drug dealing!'

While many commentators focused on what was going wrong, very few spoke of work to mitigate ethical risk and get things right. The research project therefore focused on what chairmen are doing to set and maintain the right tone from the top.

Since writing the research report, it's good to note that several initiatives have taken place to improve business ethics, especially in The City of London. Recent research has covered subjects such as Virtuous Banking, Improving Corporate Governance and People Trust and Authenticity. However, the need for better ethics remains: ethical scandals have not gone away. For example, The Royal Bank of Scotland was fined £390m for its part in the London interbank offered rate (LIBOR) rate-fixing scandal and allocated £3.2bn to compensate customers for mis-sold loan insurance. In August 2014 it was fined a further £15m for serious failings in their advised mortgage business. It was subsequently fined £56m for unacceptable computer failure. And in early 2015, RBS admitted it had been mis-selling business loans. In September 2014, Barclays was fined £37.7m for failing to protect properly, clients' safe custody assets. In fact, in a long list that mentions Lloyds, Credit Suisse, The Yorkshire Building Society, Barclays, Invesco and Santander, the Financial Conduct Authority, the UK's financial regulator, levied fines of £1,471,431,800 in 2014 (http://www.fca.org.uk/firms/being-regulated/enforcement/fines).

Perhaps poor business ethics have always been with us and human nature has not changed. What has changed is the greater transparency that exists today combined with the speed with which revelations and allegations can be made. Social media enable people to declare opinions and re-tweet them or forward them with just one touch. The court of public opinion rarely checks all the facts, as some individuals have found to their cost. But once a story is out, there is little organisations can do to defend themselves. This implies that reputation management is the new imperative – for individuals, professions and organisations. Increasingly, it appears that board nomination committees are asking executive and non-executive candidates whether there is anything, anything at all, in their past history that could embarrass the organisation.

Websites such as Glass Door enable employees to pass comment on their employer. It is very public and employees do not feel constrained by the way questions are presented in internal employee engagement surveys. Increasingly, employers are turning to Glass Door to see what employees really think and to consider how they can improve their organisation's reputation.

A company partnering with local organisations faced bribery allegations in the Far East. As the larger partner and a foreign entity, there was no escaping the spotlight. What did not make the headlines was that eight organisations were being investigated in the sector in that country and two of them were local enterprises. The authorities came down hard on the foreign company, in their own way sending a clear tone from the top of government. That sent a signal to all foreign companies trading there. It also sent a signal to local companies, saying 'This is what can happen. We are pursuing foreign companies but we can come after you too'.

The original research for this book was published by Keeldeep Associates Limited and Ashridge Business School at the end of 2013. I presented it to a variety of business audiences in a series of seminars and conferences in 2014. As a result of that, Gower Publishing asked that it be turned into a book, augmented by my own experience and observations from a 32-year career in corporate life. This book therefore comprises three parts:

Part I contains the original research, based on interviews with the chairmen of FTSE200 companies in 2013. This sets the scene using contemporary research, based on interviews with the chairmen of more than a quarter of a trillion pounds of market capitalisation. It should therefore be reasonably representative of UK plc. It also shows that no matter how big a company, its leadership must take action to mitigate ethical risk. Simply 'being vigilant' is not enough.

Part II is a collection of my observations and case studies from experience as a senior HR professional, International HR Director, Global HR Director, Group HR Director and ultimately a member of the Executive Committee of a FTSE150 public limited company. Some are attributed, others not. Some are from my direct experience, others are observations from other organisations I was aware of. They have been included to illustrate the tone from the top and its impact on effective and ineffective handling of situations.

Part III contains some observations and reflections on leadership, again taken from my own experience and observation. Having spent many years with learning and development directors working for me, I have worked closely on the design, development and delivery of leadership development programmes in corporations. Perhaps of greater use to the reader, I have also owned the strategic review of talent in a FTSE150 plc. This entailed running global talent processes and presenting succession plans to the main board. Being at the heart of who was developed and promoted gave a remarkable insight into how organisations define leadership, how the definition changes as the cast changes and which leadership attributes are valued above others.

A poor tone from the top is often a predictor of questionable or aggressive financial reporting. When companies first report negative news, there is usually more to come. At the time of writing, reports in the press about Tesco alleged that its £250m over-statement of profit expectations was the outcome of the tone of a business under pressure – a business straining too hard to deliver growth and becoming ever more willing to brush aside those who sought to interfere with its vision. Subsequently, three executives were asked to 'step aside'. That figure became five executives, then eight. A good tone from the top normally leads companies to report both good and bad news as they happen. Such openness is likely to influence shareholder actions and behaviour. Highly regarded companies all have periods of missing forecast, they suffer profit warnings and loss of market share. However, they tend to be open about where they stand and what they are doing. My contention throughout this book is that leadership's behaviour is a vital element in the tone from the top. Leaders multiply their contribution through their influence on others. A good tone – including the behavioural tone – encourages employees at all levels to speak out about malpractice, to ask for help or check before doing something questionable. Companies from Enron to *The News of the World* had a strategy. Unfortunately, the tone allowed a corporate culture to develop that ultimately overwhelmed any chance of the strategy succeeding. And that is why I believe behaviour trumps strategy.

Ian Muir

London, 2015

PART I

THE RESEARCH INTO *THE TONE FROM THE TOP*

Many companies have been criticised for weaknesses in their business ethics, including in some cases breaking the law.

In 2013, the repercussions of PPI mis-selling, of LIBOR manipulation, of Deep Water Horizon, of the horsemeat scandal and other historic problems continued to plague the companies involved. In 2014, scandals continued as did prosecutions by the regulators, especially in financial services. Company profits in affected organisations were hit, in part due to hundreds of millions of pounds set aside for compensation payments, 'customer redress' and mis-selling of inappropriate products.

But the problem of ethical lapses is not confined to business. MPs continue to be viewed with suspicion as a result of their expenses scandal. The National Health Service suffered from the Mid-Staffordshire scandal in which nurses appeared to ignore patient needs. Journalists are tarnished by the phone-hacking scandal that first surfaced at *The News of the World*. Defence procurement was alleged to be wasteful when scrutinised by the public accounts committee. Formula One motor racing was tarnished by a multi-million-euro settlement offer to avoid prosecution in Germany. There are few sectors of society that can claim the moral high ground.

This year, like every other year, new scandals and ethical breaches have hit the media. Not so long ago, Google and Amazon faced a parliamentary committee investigating their accounting practices which led to alleged very low payments of corporation tax, and Ernst & Young was held to account for advising on such practices. HSBC was fined $2bn for allowing money laundering in Central America. It was alleged that the BBC paid executives excessive compensation for loss of office and misled both internal and external audiences about the situation.

Tesco was fined for selling strawberries at 'half price' even though the period at which the strawberries were sold at full price was less than that required by law. Six furniture retailers were investigated for alleged false discounting in which no one really paid the pre-discount prices. Serco was accused of misrepresenting the number of prisoners it transported and its share price fell 14 per cent in a day. The CFO of Zurich Insurance committed suicide and left a note naming the chairman's management style; he subsequently resigned. Olympus Cameras was to be prosecuted in the UK for false accounting. Poly Implants Protheses, a French company, was accused of selling breast implants made from industrial silicone, a fuel additive and chemicals used in the production of industrial rubber tubing.

We live in a much more transparent world. The implication is that ethical issues are commonplace. As a result, all boards need to think carefully about how they give ethical leadership to their companies.

The objective of this research was to understand how boards provide ethical leadership; how boards monitor the tone that they are setting; and how non-executive directors check that their company has a good ethical compass. The research also sought to identify examples of good practice.

The research and report were completed by Ian Muir, Director at Keeldeep Associates, and sponsored by Ashridge Business School. The research elicited the views of a range of mostly FTSE100 and FTSE250 chairmen – from diverse sectors including energy, engineering, pharmaceuticals, retail, professional services, construction, hospitality, infrastructure development and financial services.

Some interviewees chair more than one company and many are on more than one board. I am grateful to all the contributors for their candid views and advice, based on their experience and learning.

THE PARTICIPANTS

The chairmen of the following companies are thanked for their participation in this research. In the case of other organisations, the most senior representative is also thanked for their participation. All were generous with their time and gave many helpful insights. Where individuals are on more than one board, they usually responded with perspectives from all companies. Where there was comment from other organisations, this is mentioned as being from the wider stakeholder group.

Associated British Foods plc
BAE Systems plc
Balfour Beatty plc
Barratt Developments plc
Beazley plc
BG Group plc
Bodycote plc
Capital and Counties Properties plc
Compass Group plc
DS Smith plc
Ecclesiastical Insurance plc
GlaxoSmithKline plc
Greggs plc
Hays plc
Howden Joinery Group plc
ICAP plc
Informa plc
Laird plc
Morrisons plc
National Grid plc
NextiraOne BV
Old Mutual plc
Page Group plc
Schroders plc
Standard Life plc
Tate & Lyle plc

William Hill plc
Wincanton plc
Wolseley plc

Association of British Insurers
Institute for Business Ethics
MWM Consulting

EXECUTIVE SUMMARY OF THE RESEARCH: BOARDS SHOULD SET A TONE FROM THE TOP

Chairmen and their boards recognise the importance of the tone from the top. But, some see it as more than just business ethics. For them, 'tone' is also about performance expectations. This report, however, focuses on the business ethics element of the tone from the top and describes the findings from the interviews. Appendix 1 contains a seven-step model for managing ethical risk derived from the interviews.

All interviewees acknowledged the vital role of good business ethics. Many had personal examples to discuss in which actions in their companies had fallen below acceptable standards, so all recognised the need for assurance processes and for the board to send the right signals. Moreover, most chairmen feel they are still learning. While most are comfortable with their board's approach to compliance, there are big differences in the processes chairmen are using for ethical assurance. Also, there is no obvious best practice on how to deliver signals to the organisation about how managers should behave. Only a few of the participants appeared to have a structured holistic framework for addressing the challenge of setting an appropriate 'tone from the top'.

ETHICAL RISK CANNOT BE ELIMINATED

Ethical risk is like commercial risk. It cannot be fully eliminated. All companies will have some of the following:

- 'Bad apples' – people with inappropriate morals
- 'Foolish or incompetent apples' – people who unthinkingly do the wrong thing
- 'Tempted apples' – people who are in a situation that pressures or tempts them to do the wrong thing

While boards have a choice of how much commercial risk they want to incur, they should try to minimise ethical risk. They can do this by strengthening recruitment and assessment processes to minimise the number of bad apples, training people to reduce the number of foolish apples and building moral backbone to reduce the number of pressured apples. While this report is mainly about the findings from the research, a framework is offered in Appendix 1 to help boards with a more holistic approach to managing their tone from the top.

A GOOD TONE STARTS WITH A GOOD BOARD

Good boards are made by good chairmen. So the starting point is a chairman with strong professional skills and high ethical standards. The chairman then needs to ensure there is a strong board. If executives respect the board, the signals the board gives will have more effect and will have more traction further down the organisation.

STRONG GOVERNANCE IS PART OF TONE FROM THE TOP

Executives need to feel that the board is interested and knowledgeable and is likely to find out what is going on one way or the other. This requires strong processes of governance and reporting, and board members who take the time to walk the business, meet the managers and have an open dialogue between executives and non-executives. Boards should be particularly sensitive to:

- Lack of transparency or a lack of information around critical decisions
- Failure by the executive or non-executives to confront difficult issues
- Adversarial interpersonal relationships or an atmosphere that makes it hard to air concerns
- Over-reliance on process rather than open dialogue

THE TONE MUST BE LED BY THE CEO

The board cannot replace the CEO in setting the tone. The board's role is to support the CEO. The board can demonstrate the importance of good ethics by devoting time to the topic. The board can help the CEO with difficult decisions. The board can also check that the CEO is using all the levers at his or her disposal both to communicate the importance of good ethics and to assess actual behaviour.

THE LEVERS OF TONE FROM THE TOP

The interviews uncovered a long list of the levers that CEOs and boards are using to help manage the tone from the top:

- Risk assessments: some companies seek to identify situations where bad ethical choices are likely to be most damaging to the company – for example information submitted to a regulator for a utility, or product quality for a branded company
- Recruitment selection processes: companies are finding additional ways of assessing the ethical compass of new recruits and senior appointments, such as taking references from their previous finance executives
- Board sub-committees: boards are setting up sub-committees or renaming sub-committees to signal the board's commitment to business ethics
- Employee survey processes: companies are designing questions for the employee survey to assess the state of ethics in different parts of their organisations. Some are using these to set individual targets for managers
- Whistleblowing: companies are strengthening their whistleblowing policies, by, for example, putting the telephone number on the back of lavatory doors
- Informal intelligence: non-executives are increasingly looking for opportunities to 'walk the business' and meet executives in informal contexts
- Ethical breach reports: some boards are calling for a regular report of ethical breaches, disciplinary consequences, learnings from breaches and communication processes around breaches
- Codes of conduct: companies are using their codes of conduct to help signal their commitment, by, for example, asking all executives to sign the code each year
- Values and training: companies use values and training to reinforce their ethical code and build a stronger moral backbone in the company
- External audits: companies are beginning to use external audits of ethical behaviour and policies to signal commitment and to demonstrate performance
- Incentive and reward processes: companies are reviewing their incentive processes to identify situations where temptations or pressures may cause their people to behave out of character. Claw-back is becoming more common
- Assessment processes: companies are adding moral character to their performance appraisals
- Business relationships: companies are looking carefully at all of their business relationships, particularly where a business partner may have different values.

THERE ARE NO SILVER BULLETS

None of the chairmen interviewed believe that there are simple answers to the challenge of setting the tone from the top. Moreover, with a crowded agenda of compliance and business issues, it may not be appropriate to attempt to add extra items to board meetings on business ethics. Hence, the challenge seems to be about finding levers that help communicate a high tone from the top without crowding out time for dialogue about the business.

KEY MESSAGES FOR EACH STAKEHOLDER GROUP

Chairmen should have a holistic approach and a systematic strategy for business ethics.

Chairmen

- Assemble and develop a first class board; be clear about skill requirements
- Assess your ethical risks – identify where unethical behaviour could do the most damage
- Consider how best to set the ethical tone and send clear signals to the organisation about the standards and behaviours that are expected
- Make the best use of both input measures (what is being done to reduce external risk) and output measures (are employees acting ethically?)
- Check the CEO has processes in place to assure ethical compliance

Senior Independent Directors

- Ask questions about your management and the board's strategy for setting a good ethical tone
- Encourage the chairman to follow through on process and behavioural issues

Non-executive Directors

- Show courage to be independent, especially regarding ethical issues
- Develop relationships with executives below the board without undermining the CEO
- Ask for output measures such as employee survey results and data on ethical breaches

Executive Directors

- Encourage the CEO to provide strong ethical leadership
- Ensure learning from ethics breaches is captured, communicated and used well
- Recognise that when investors ask companies to 'comply or explain', they base their opinions on the quality and alignment of responses coming from the Chairman and the CEO

HR Directors

- Coach board members on how behavioural signals are being interpreted
- Push for learning and feedback mechanisms that will help to enhance ethical behaviour
- Ensure that performance management, engagement and succession processes measure ethical matters

Regulators

- Be prepared to discuss ethical issues with companies
- Encourage companies to measure their ethical performance

Investors

- Look for companies that have a strong ethical tone: they should be less risky investments

THE RESPONSES AND FINDINGS

Chairmen recognise that board decisions and behaviour have a big impact lower down the organisation. They also recognise that the CEO must be the prime driver of the tone from the top. Most, however, did not appear to have a fully systematic approach to ethics.

1: THE VITAL ROLE OF A STRONG BOARD

The foundation of a strong board is a professionally strong chairman, whose untouchable integrity and leadership style set the tone for how the board works. Chairmen and external commentators recognise that the job of the Chairman has become more complex, making it even more important that the chairman's instincts about tone are appropriate.

The next requirement for a strong board is the quality of the directors. Chairmen are actively upgrading their boards and updating the skills represented. One chairman said he is extremely rigorous about board composition. He conducts a skills assessment of the board and uses a skills matrix orientated to future skill requirements. No one can be appointed to any of the group's boards without being interviewed by him. Moreover, he believes that a new face every one or two years enables that company to raise its game and avoid 'groupthink':

> *Every one or two years we have new board members. They have eyes and ears. They go out and about which helps set the tone in a very real way.*

Increasingly, chairmen believe that emotional intelligence is needed to pick the right board and to run it effectively:

> *Board members provide ethical leadership by who they are. It is transparent very quickly what really matters to them. One transmits ethical leadership via the quality of interaction.*

Chairmen should also encourage good open relations between non-executive directors and executives:

> *All our companies have an active NED visit programme unaccompanied by people from the centre.*

The importance of the CEO, however, is clear. The CEO is the leader. He or she drives the ethical culture through the organisation. However, there appears to be a growing sense of partnership with the board:

> *Boards are forging closer links to the business, including a bigger sounding board with the CEO. Good CEOs are thinking "What expertise can I draw from the board?"*

2: STRONG GOVERNANCE IS A PREREQUISITE

Good governance is seen as the starting point. During the interviews there was no debate about the importance of UK Governance Code points, such as good reporting, well-designed decision-making, truly independent directors, clearly delegated authorities, effective audit, risk and corporate responsibility committees and so on. The concept of 'comply or explain' was also well understood and supported.

Several chairmen spoke of improvements made to their governance structures. It is noteworthy that according to New Bridge Street Consultants, fewer remuneration reports were 'red-topped' or voted down in the 2013 and 2014 reporting seasons.

Beyond the UK Governance Code, many companies also have the ethics basics in place. These include ethics policies, codes of conduct, values statements, whistleblowing policies and site visits. But, as chairmen pointed out, it is the way these tools are used that is more important than their existence:

> *We monitor every whistleblowing report. This is an important part of our board reporting. We monitor health and safety as a surrogate for good management. ... We monitor the number of quality awards we receive because we see an absolute correlation between leadership of a division and the number of awards.*

In applying the tools in a more systematic way, boards are aiming for wider and deeper understanding throughout their companies. For example, it was felt by several chairmen that, where the different tools of ethical governance are well communicated, employees are more likely to know which tool to use and how to raise issues or concerns. Similarly, managers are more open to such issues being raised. Feedback loops are also being used to help drive continuous improvement.

Many governance structures had previously been more federal or 'hands-off'. Now boards are more involved with operations. For example, some chairmen described programmes in which board members act as ambassadors for ethics across the world. Chairmen recognise the danger of going too far and of stepping on the CEO's toes. So there is a delicate balance to be found between an active board and an executive team who are fully in charge:

> *We attach high importance to identity and culture. The board didn't have to push on these topics. It's part of our DNA. We are actively trying to make it more than just sentences in the annual report and accounts. Our staff are widely dispersed. The board agrees culture and values. We have active engagement with the executive and our NEDs attend site visits and meetings with high potential middle ranking executives worldwide.*

For the companies participating in this research, the following tables show the percentage using various tools. They have been separated into input measures (what is being done to reduce ethical risks) and output measures (are employees acting ethically?).

Input measures

	% of companies
The company has a set of values	85
The company has a code of conduct	100
The company trains its people in the values	77
The company trains its people in its code of conduct	96
The company trains people regularly in ethical matters	85
The company evaluates its people for their ethics or adherence to the company values	81
The company has a whistleblowing policy	100
The company conducts occasional ethics audits	35
There are questions on ethics and values in the employee survey	77

Output measures

	% of companies
Outcomes from employee surveys inform board action	88
Individual manager targets are determined from employee surveys	52
Managers with less than perfect ratings on ethics and values are tracked	48
The number of ethical incidents is tracked	92
The locations/countries/business units with ethical incidents are tracked	92
Results from ethical audits are reported	35
The amount and value of business turned away due to ethical concerns is tracked	48

These tables reinforce the view that the basics are largely in place. However, the extent and frequency of employee training in ethics shows room for improvement. Many boards use data from compliance programmes (such as training on anti-bribery and corruption, codes of conduct and whistleblowing) but only half used the data to direct individual targets for managers – such as for environment, health and safety, engagement and quality awards.

Only half of boards are monitoring the percentage of managers who score less than perfect ethical ratings in the appraisal process. Similarly, only about half are monitoring the amount and value of business turned away as a result of ethical concerns. Only a third appear to be conducting ethics audits.

Few chairmen presented their use of tools as part of a holistic approach involving both input and output measures designed to improve overall ethical leadership. Hence the distinction between input and output measures may be an example of good practice.

Generally, the larger FTSE100 companies appeared to have more comprehensive use of ethics tools. This may reflect the fact that larger companies have more resources. However, one chairman said the strength of resolve from the top is ultimately much more important than the cost:

> *Too often boards get involved in processes and clutch cards, presentations and so on but along the way they get lost. If you ask "who are we, what's distinctive and who do we want to be?" that is good guidance. The CEO must be comfortable communicating the outputs. It's about distinctiveness and asking: Is it real?*

Few chairmen have received formal feedback from shareholders on the tone from the top. One company had received comment that its values were seen as part of the investment case. Generally, however, the view was that shareholder bodies form opinions based on the quality of aligned responses coming from the chairman and CEO. Some chairmen felt few external bodies wanted to give praise for fear of future problems coming back to haunt them.

3: SPECIAL ATTENTION TO ETHICS IS INCREASING

Several chairmen spoke of their governance structures and moral oversight in the same sentence. One chairman researched his company's ethics code and compliance at the top. On discovering that not all board members were bound by it, he made changes. Now the whole board is fully 'signed-up' in both the letter and spirit of the code.

Some chairmen had done research to identify where their companies face the greatest ethical risk. Others were stimulated more by responding to internal and external events, such as the Bribery Act or an internal fraud or mis-selling breach.

Several chairmen spoke of the importance of product quality, supplier integrity and accurate representation of the organisation to outsiders:

> *Be very clear on what you are. Debate what's most relevant within the wider consideration of ethics. What we intend to be for our customers: honest, fair, never misrepresenting, assured product provenance, how you treat your people. Honesty, transparency and fair dealing.*

One company would not do business with the West Bank for the supply of products. Health and safety issues regarding anything in the food chain were high on the agenda, particularly in light of recent scandals such as the appearance of horsemeat in prepared meals. Several chairmen mentioned transparent pricing as a key part of public trust in organisations. This followed reports of Tesco being fined £300,000 plus £65,000 costs for misrepresenting strawberries as being 'half-price'.

Defining what's important enables boards to focus. By shifting the spotlight of attention from time to time, they are able to keep ethics firmly on the agenda. This helps to avoid 'initiative fatigue':

> *What we expect is set out in various documents in the public domain. But we have to go further than that with visible action – taking the lead.*

The challenge now is how to keep our programme alive, several years after the original driver for change. We have to do this through continuous improvement.

Chairmen are spending more time with CEOs on ethics. This is easier where the relationship is strong. Many chairmen felt taking a 'diagonal slice' through the company to measure the effectiveness of ethics programmes was helpful. Discussing the outputs from employee surveys with the CEO was one way of keeping the dialogue alive.

While there is an acknowledged challenge for non-executive directors to judge whether their companies are putting enough effort into ethical leadership, boards appear to be spending more time on ethical matters. Boards also appear to be asking more follow-on questions whenever they have ethical concerns:

The tone comes from the board. I meet the CEO every week or two. I assess the quality of the relationship: is it too cosy or are issues swept under the table? Are there unresolved issues?

Each ethical subject has a compliance and risk review. It's a very thorough process. Not only the board but each business unit reviews ethics.

What boards do with the information they get from employee surveys or other tools was instructive. Best practice includes using trend analysis to pinpoint areas for action and topics to be refreshed. It also includes using the data to set personal targets for business unit heads, divisional heads, department heads and even individual managers.

Communications around ethical issues are becoming more transparent. For example fewer departures that are the result of bad behaviour are glossed over. Increasingly, when a senior person leaves, the real reason is given.

Some chairmen went beyond process and audit and described more subtle measures and actions:

We see three lines of defence: who you put in charge; processes and audit functions; wider governance and feedback.

We have a strong internal audit function. We rotate some of our best people through internal audit. They are admired and highly respected.

While you have to rely on the effectiveness of the processes, education and training, one also tends to home-in when things go wrong. Whistleblowing, profit, safety or regulatory surprises. Or the sniff test. Auditors are sometimes the last to highlight subtle issues as they don't always have great seniority, breadth and emotional intelligence.

One chairman described how the annual employee engagement survey was used to monitor the climate at local offices. His organisation picks up issues and involves staff in rectifying them. After four or five years the survey was felt to be fully embedded and a good safeguard.

One recurring topic was the increasing emphasis on contact with operational management. In my 2012 report, *Board Evaluation*, the area where chairmen felt they had made the most progress was 'Contact with people below the board'. When asked where progress was most needed for the coming year, they gave the same answer. It appears that, increasingly, chairmen and NEDs want to see at first hand the calibre of management:

> *We have HQ representation on all our subsidiary boards. We have clear criteria for delegation.*

> *The NEDs are free to go anywhere in the company: any committee, any question, any product review board. And they do attend; the Executive welcomes it. My attendance at certain management meetings helps me see the talent and what their attitudes are.*

4: THERE IS GROWING AWARENESS OF THE IMPLICATIONS OF SIGNALLING

Chairmen recognise the power and importance of signalling by the board through its actions.

Renaming board sub-committees or setting up new sub-committees sends strong signals to management:

> *There was no corporate responsibility committee when I arrived. Now there is absolute commitment from the board. ... You have to ensure the right board composition. It helps to do something dramatic to focus the ethical compass.*

One organisation appointed a highly respected outsider to conduct an independent review of its practices. From the outset, the chairman committed to implement all the recommendations – sight unseen. That sent a clear signal regarding priorities and importance.

Some chairmen sent explicit signals by undertaking the same training as all employees on ethics, codes of conduct, whistleblowing and anti-bribery and corruption law. They felt this showed how boards are 'walking the talk'. Those chairmen wanted to show they treat the subject seriously and if the training is good enough for them, it should be good enough throughout the company.

One chairman spoke of the tacit signalling from who gets appointed and, more importantly, who is *not* appointed to senior jobs. Others spoke of more overt signalling when dealing with bad behaviour:

> *It was generally assumed that one executive was the obvious choice for a key promotion. It was expected. However we had some residual questions and we decided to appoint someone else whose ethics were beyond reproach. That sent a clear signal and it was widely talked about.*

> *You have to set an example when managing the worst habits of some individuals. Bad behaviour means "he's going" even if the person is a high revenue earner. People need to personalise it and ask how they would feel if it was in their family.*

> *You have to have zero tolerance and make examples.*

Almost all the chairmen have increased the number of operational site visits and the number of board meetings that take place outside head office. They use these opportunities to interact with management in different settings, giving the board opportunities to learn and to influence:

> *The board has three meetings a year in the operations and more than half the time is spent with the business unit people. What the board does and thinks are important.*

Boards are acutely aware of the importance of signalling to newly acquired companies. As the number of M&A transactions recovers, this was seen as a key area of focus. Effort is however required to ensure the signalling is aligned, authentic and effective:

> *Authenticity is vital. The agenda must be endorsed by the whole board. If safety is the number one issue, one must avoid lip service. Make it real. Fake signalling is worse than no signalling.*

Chairmen are mindful of the increasing spotlight on business ethics and the opportunity to send signals through board changes. Boards and especially chairmen are paying much greater attention to how they appoint new members:

> *I don't want to imply causation regarding ethics but we have appointed a new CFO, some new NEDs and a new CEO over recent years. It's not that*

there were problems but we do have better people now. They set a better constructively challenging tone – including by their behaviour.

The real point is how you behave when ethically challenged. That is when your actions are tested.

Tone from the top is not a motivational crusade. Most changes happen where there are doubts about whether the tone is the right one. Ultimately chairmen should change the CEO if the values and ethics aren't present to the right extent.

Another way to signal is by the board's reactions to events. One company was involved with suppliers who were using premises that suffered a catastrophic building collapse. Despite some legalistic arguments to the contrary, the board showed leadership by providing cash, food and medicine to affected families. There was a strong ethical sense of 'We will do the right thing' from the chairman:

Culture emanates from the boardroom. It changes as the board changes. A dysfunctional board is lethal.

This quote illustrates the level of emotional commitment and sense of responsibility felt by one chairman. He saw his ethics and behaviour influencing the tone of the whole board.

Attention to corporate values is another source of signalling. Interestingly only half the interviewees specifically mentioned values and the signals these send. Those who did mentioned culture emanating from the boardroom and saw that as a clear signalling opportunity.

5: DIFFERENT APPROACHES MAY BE RELEVANT ACCORDING TO A COMPANY'S STAGE OF DEVELOPMENT

Founder-dominated companies can encounter specific challenges if the founder's ethics are not aligned with those of the board. If the founder is still in the business, it can be difficult to change the status quo. Some chairmen spoke of the professionalising of boards in companies where founders had moved on.

There were several examples where a history of previous family ownership had inculcated a strong, enduring company culture. Chairmen spoke of values-led organisations they admired. Some, however, added that it was difficult to conserve those values in a large plc and through growth by acquisition.

Chairmen also spoke of the importance of harmonising governance structures when acquiring and integrating companies. One spoke of the challenge of making tacit knowledge more explicit after acquiring a company with a different culture. The acquired culture was more orientated towards execution based on explicit instruction. This contrasted with the pre-existing more intuitive culture based on long-term experience and guidance.

Chairmen of smaller companies felt they had fewer resources to drive compliance and behaviour. One smaller company chairman felt the ethical focus may be different depending on a company's stage of development. In addition to universal ethical practices, the ethical focus for a start-up should also pay particular attention to growth and how it is being achieved. For a company in crisis it should be exceptionally focused. For a more mature company it should ensure its ethical processes are complete and effective:

> Sometimes you need to step back and consider whether the tone is right for the current circumstances. One needs to be acutely alert to what is going on. The governance processes must include informal observation.

There is a need for vigilance in situations where economic pressures may cloud people's judgement. For example, if profits fall dramatically in a recession, extra emphasis may be required to ensure sales are booked correctly to the appropriate accounting period. Redundancies should be undertaken with integrity and fair process; separation payments should be correct and compliant with policy as well as the law. They should not be enhanced above the recipient's entitlement, as the BBC learned to its cost.

6: REDUCING THE NUMBER OF 'BAD APPLES'

It is impossible to have no 'bad apples' in large organisations. However, paying particular attention to three things can help mitigate the risk. Those areas are: selection processes, performance management and the whistleblowing process.

Selection processes: hiring people at all levels increasingly includes an assessment of candidates' honesty, integrity and ethics. Due diligence and reference checking are being done more thoroughly, especially at senior levels. In addition, chairmen spoke of enquiries into people's reputations. Consideration of a candidate may go beyond subjects directly related to jobs and can extend to family and financial matters. Also, head-hunters are making more informal calls to take soundings among a wider pool.

Performance management: some organisations consider their performance appraisal processes lack teeth. Chairmen were mindful of the need for candour and straight talking when evaluating board members and senior line managers. There appears to be an opportunity for even greater candour by putting an ethical assessment into performance review processes.

Whistleblowing processes: while all the companies participating in this research have whistleblowing policies, the way they are implemented and brought to life makes a difference to their effectiveness. One chairman spoke of publicity for the whistleblowing contact number. Rather than having this only on noticeboards where employees might be frightened of being seen writing it down in a public area, posters were also placed on the inside of lavatory cubicle doors.

7: REDUCING THE NUMBER OF 'FOOLISH APPLES'

Chairmen recognised that sometimes employees at any level can do foolish things. They felt that communicating values was a helpful way of reducing inappropriate actions and behaviour. These provide the context for situations where there are no explicit rules. Some commented on the power of signalling to underline the context. For example, significant disciplinary action such as a dismissal for improper conduct helps others understand the line they should not cross:

> The audit committee receives reports on why people are fired. We report this
> in our CSR reports.

Chairmen spoke about educating and training their employees so that they would be able to raise concerns with confidence. One said he hoped that such programmes reached sufficiently deep into the company that on the last working day of an accounting period, a shop-floor employee would not send out a consignment to inflate the period-end results. Instead, he hoped they would raise the issue, ask questions and feel supported in doing the right thing when declining to ship the product. Others said that e-learning programmes could generate useful audit reports to show by department, unit and company how much and how successfully ethics and compliance training was being done. The e-learning reports could be used to focus attention on areas with weak training completion rates, areas of poor compliance and areas of significant risk:

> We have exhaustive training programmes and sign-off showing completion.

One organisation discovered that inaccurate information had been provided to an external third party. This was an example of foolish behaviour from an employee who received no personal gain from their action, yet the consequences were significant. This led to reviews of the importance and significance of information flows, who is authorised to approve external submissions and what the reputational risks might be. The company concluded that it needed to monitor and control information flows where the risk is high:

> We review our reporting, key ratios and comparison with best practice. We also work at what is the critical information, which if wrong, would cause huge reputational risk or financial risk. We have to have confidence that the assurance mechanisms are fit for purpose. If data is important, it cannot be self-certified. External third party certification may be needed.

8: REDUCING THE NUMBER OF 'TEMPTED APPLES'

While there has been good progress in process compliance (whistleblowing policy, code of conduct and the role of the audit committee), there is more to be done to create a systemic culture. For example, while many companies have a published set of values, more could be done to train and assess people on their adherence to the values.

Few chairmen spoke of mapping out situations in the business that could give rise to tempting and/or pressured situations. There is a clear opportunity to identify and highlight pressured/tempting situations. Where these exist, the processes, such as incentives and performance appraisal, may need to be reviewed and extra training may be necessary.

Linking the identification and analysis of tempting situations with signalling opportunities from the board is another opportunity to reduce the risk of temptation:

> Sometimes you have to be quite directive. The board must show its flag: this is how we operate. We always talk about this at our conferences: this is the way we operate with suppliers and vendors. We all complete the register of corporate entertainment and gifts.

In another situation a code of conduct was launched by members of the executive committee, who spoke with passion about ethical dilemmas they had faced:

> The code of conduct was a game changer. It is the only document that goes to every employee worldwide. It's about identity. A different way of talking about things. We had a strong launch – with ExCo members talking about their ethics.

Referring to corruption in some countries, one chairman spoke of the importance of investing in high-quality local management. Joint ventures can be particularly challenging, especially if the joint venture partner does not share the same ethical views. While audit committees have largely 'cracked' formal and process issues in advanced countries, the focus is being increased in emerging markets. Another chairman spoke of the risk of being a more visible partner; several said they chose not to operate in certain countries.

Sometimes, events can lead to quite radical solutions to reduce future risk:

> *We had some petty fraud. As a result, we outsourced internal audit and it was the best thing we have done. There is no hiding place. The provider takes a very professional, continuous audit approach. This picks up unusual things. It's much better. It is important to show you have done something about the issues that arise.*

Some chairmen spoke of reward structures and the need to reduce temptation by not rewarding short-term performance. One said that when it comes to allocating bonuses, there is a thorough review process to ensure appropriate allocation to the right people. In some cases, bonus payments are subject to certain governance assurance hurdles. For example, if business success was achieved but environmental or health and safety performance was inadequate, there would be a material reduction in bonus payments. In addition, in some organisations, the 'how' of performance was reviewed as well as the 'what'. If there was significant collateral damage, then bonuses would be reduced or withheld. Increasingly, the provision for bonus claw-backs is being written into incentive schemes for executives below the board:

> *We were the first in our sector to use claw-back to institutionalise a sharper focus.*

> *There should be clear examples of what happens if people misbehave. They should either have their bonus removed or be fired. Applying pure logic doesn't really work. Everyone knows what they ought to do. Some people can be a saint for 364 days a year but then on the 365th, the use of inappropriate words or conduct can cause a problem. Whatever processes are in place, if the culture is wrong people will get round the rules.*

One chairman commented on the UBS trader in 'synthetic equity derivatives', saying that the job title should have given a clue that no one really knew what he was doing. Poor controls had led to temptation. In contrast, he said the following:

> *We check to see whether a division has issues – high labour turnover, whistleblowing and so on. Reorganisations can sometimes signal poor management.*

How companies learn from ethical breaches was not uppermost in the discussions. It appears that few companies have well-organised formal processes to capture the learning from past breaches and from breaches in other organisations and then to apply that learning to reduce temptation.

9: WHAT GETS IN THE WAY

Overall, chairmen were confident and optimistic about their ability to provide a good tone from the top. However, some things do impede progress. One said that addressing poor behaviour in a high-performing company requires strength and bravery from the Chair. If there is insufficient challenge and behaviour is sub-optimal, ultimately performance dips.

If the quality of relationship between the board and CEO is poor, that can send dysfunctional signals and dilute the tone from the top. While people lower down the organisation have little awareness of what happens at the board, they do receive and act upon subtle signals, largely because they want to 'get on'. The CEO's approach to the tone from the top is therefore significant. For example, companies that develop a 'Good news only' culture can find it difficult to raise concerns:

> Once a CEO has run a division, a business unit or an entire business for a few years, the business tends to reflect the CEO's personality.

Chairmen expressed confidence that training on ethical matters was effective and from a process perspective there was clear evidence of this. However upon further investigation, sometimes employees were sceptical, thinking that they were having to do a lot of compliance work to make amends for shortcomings among senior people:

> Some employees felt "We are having to do all this to make you look good".

Testing to see whether organisations have their employees' hearts as well as their heads was considered useful and the best route was via the employee survey:

> Our improved operating model gives more insight and oversight without micro-management. The ethical survey is used to bring business units closer together.

> The most important part of the employee survey is on the ethical questions. The board reviews the survey. There are individual manager targets fed in via the performance review process.

One chairman felt that top management and the front line were committed but that sometimes middle management was not committed. One commented that over-engineered solutions could become a challenge for implementation by managers:

We over-engineered the response to the external advisory report. It contained 23 principles which were seen as dictats.

Doing business in different countries can bring ethical challenges, particularly in joint ventures. If there is corruption in a country, the quality of local management may fall below the ethical standards set by one of the partners:

JVs have been difficult because local partners have not bought into this ethical stuff. The emerging markets are harder. We are very cautious in getting the right management.

In the event of problems, the larger partner will be the one held to account. We now live in a totally different world. Social networking and the internet make communication and criticism instantaneous, making it harder for companies to defend themselves.

If the Chair and NED's tone was diluted by the executive, that would cause a problem that required action. The board has to be very careful that safety, environment and health receive the same attention as the financial results.

The politically correct element is a distraction and some people can get carried away. You can't build a great business without ethical standards. Good companies do it because it is a good way to operate.

10: ADVICE FROM THE PARTICIPANTS

The most frequent advice to other boards emphasised the role of the chairman as crucial to setting, upholding, maintaining and extending the tone from the top. All recognised that persistence is required:

Look into yourself. You are always on show. Behaviour is never private. Individuals project the image and reputation of the company.

Regarding mergers and acquisitions, several chairmen advised caution, saying companies should expand cautiously and should put their own people in if they can. Finding proper management can be a struggle when they are under pressure to deliver profits and cash. Building a group of managers with the right culture from the centre was therefore considered important:

Live it. You have to live it. If the troops realise you are not serious – you've lost it. If bad behaviour warrants dismissal, you have to stick to it no matter who it is. Stick to what you say.

My NEDs are pretty experienced. They are a diverse group who go see and smell the coffee to check reality. We talk to all the managers. I'd be uncomfortable if the Executive weren't happy about NEDs meeting managers without the Exec present.

All chairmen recognised the pivotal nature of their role:

Recognise the power and criticality of the tone from the top. It starts with the chair not the CEO. When things get horrible, as they sometimes do, without the chair reflecting the values, the CEO and the board will wobble. And that is very dangerous.

Send clear signals into the organisation regarding what the board thinks is important. Actions speak louder than words.

In a company with a strong values system, it's fine if it is performing well. If there is a big change – do the values allow you to do what's needed in different economic circumstances?

Boards should allow enough time for free thinking. They can sometimes get stuck in the agenda without thinking. It's amazing what comes out of discussion.

CONCLUSIONS AND REFLECTIONS ON THE RESEARCH

Most employees in large organisations have little direct contact with senior executives or board members. Their perceptions of ethical leadership are likely to be indirect, coming from symbolic behaviour, communication (verbal and non-verbal), policies and images. The perception of ethical leadership can be very subjective. However, from my own observation as a former executive committee member of a FTSE150 plc, I have met many employees who have observed and remembered with intense detail even the shortest, most fleeting interactions with top executives. Hallmarks of ethical leaders who set an appropriate tone from the top include: openness, courage, an ability to listen, honesty and fair mindedness. All of these help employees to believe that leadership is acting in the employees' best interests.

The leadership role of the chair is vital in setting the board's tone from the top. A strong, professional chair who develops a strong, professional ethical board is likely to be respected by the executives. Respected boards are likely to have more traction in setting and promulgating the tone from the top. Where there are high-quality relationships, it is more likely that boards are safe places to air problems rather than 'good news' cultures. Where there is an environment of fair, effective challenge and support, boards are more likely to be able to maximise their signalling power. This can be done through many channels.

Overt signalling can be via what's on the agenda and by showing what's important. It also comes from decisions and actions including who gets selected, developed, promoted and fired. More subtle signalling comes from how boards interact with executives and managers. It also comes from what is not said and who is not appointed. Above all, it comes from consistency and transparency, including clear delineation between the roles of the chair and CEO. The Chairman runs the board, the CEO runs the company. Companies with a strong tone from the top often have a strong culture, frequently based on values – whether formally articulated or not.

Values give guidance where there are no rules. They enable employees at all levels to consider what to do and how to behave in new and difficult situations. They enable people to speak up and speak out, provided there is a culture of allowing and encouraging this.

Boards should develop relationships with management below the board but without damaging relationships with the CEO. 'Eyes in, fingers out' is a helpful motto.

Increasingly, boards appreciate that compliance with ethics programmes – whistleblowing, codes of conduct and training – is not enough. Reducing the number of 'bad apples', 'foolish apples' and reducing temptation of susceptible people: 'tempted apples' requires more. The tone from the top is a channel for displaying ethical behaviour in ways that maximise signalling to the organisation. Appendix 1 contains a seven-step model for reducing ethical risk. Widely distributed ethical leadership, stemming from the tone from the top, helps boards multiply their message. The tone from the top also sets the psychological climate that enables employees to raise concerns. In this way, companies stand a greater chance of mitigating risk by reducing significantly the number of 'bad apples', foolish ones and those who may give in to temptation.

A SYSTEMATIC APPROACH FOR MANAGING ETHICAL RISKS

Ethical risk comes from a number of sources:

1. 'Bad apples' – individuals whose ethical compass is distorted or defective.
2. 'Foolish or incompetent apples' – individuals who do not think sufficiently or are not sufficiently trained before acting or who are fitting in with what they think is the norm.
3. 'Pressured or tempted apples' – these are situations where people act inappropriately because they are under pressure or temptation.

It is impossible to eliminate ethical risk. What is important is that the board signals that ethical behaviour is essential and puts in place assurance processes that will help to reduce the risks, especially in important areas.

THE BASICS (STEPS 1–3)

Having a CEO who believes that business ethics are important is fundamental to the following seven-step model. Unless the CEO's commitment is clear and evident, the model is unlikely to succeed.

Step 1 is to have an ethically sound chairman who knows how to select and lead a strong board. If executives respect the board, the signals the board gives will be stronger and gain greater traction.

Step 2 is to have ethically sound executives and non-executives, whose behaviour signals the board's commitment to high ethical standards.

Step 3 is to have strong governance processes that make executives feel as though the board and each layer of management are interested, knowledgeable, want to provide guidance and are likely to find out what is going on one way or another.

The ethical tone is only part of a larger strategic and performance tone. The board needs to be clear about what it is asking the executives to achieve, one part of which is to act with integrity and sound ethics. A focus on performance should not crowd out a willingness to discuss ethical issues. Equally, governance and ethics should not constrain the time available for discussing performance and business matters.

STEP 4: SIGNALLING

There are many ways in which the board can send signals. The most powerful signals come from the behaviour, language and actions of executive directors, particularly the CEO. If the CEO is sending signals that business is a game where fouling is OK if the referee does not see you (think football) or that cutting corners is acceptable to deliver results, no amount of 'good tone' from the rest of the board will have much impact.

Opportunities to signal include:

- the naming of sub-committees
- membership of sub-committees, for example is the CEO on the CSR and Ethics Committee?
- appointments and communication around appointments
- agenda items, for example disciplinary and ethical breaches reports
- attention given to codes of conduct, values, training and employee surveys
- board training sessions – boards can have values training too
- external ethical audits
- information requests, for example about ethical breaches
- decisions and communication around ethical breaches
- symbolic actions that communicate a commitment to do the right thing, such as compensating customers/suppliers who have suffered through no fault of their own

To maximise the signalling power of board action, the board can pick an area of focus (or possibly two). It is unreasonable to try to cover everything, and the act of focusing allows the board to do a really thorough job in the chosen area, rather than having a once-over-lightly approach across a range of issues. By doing a thorough job, the board can signal that it is prepared to walk its talk. If well chosen and well communicated, the focus acts as a symbol of the board's commitment to integrity and ethics. It also enables the board to refresh the message, by choosing a new area of focus after a few years.

For many companies, safety is a perfect lead issue to focus on. For financial services companies it might be sales integrity. For a consulting company, it might be 'clients come first'. The chosen lead issue is likely to be one of the values of the company. Ideally it should be the one that is most important.

STEP 5: ASSURANCE: REDUCING THE RISK OF 'BAD APPLES'

The board can monitor risk through input measures (what is being done to reduce ethical risks) and output measures (are employees acting ethically?). It can be helpful to distinguish between risks from 'bad apples', 'foolish apples' and 'pressured apples'. Some of the levers for reducing risk are helpful across all three types of risk.

The main focus for reducing the risk of 'bad apples' should be selection and assessment processes. The best way to reduce the risk is to reduce the number of employees whose ethics are inappropriate. Input measures include:

- whether recruitment and appointment processes include an assessment of ethics and the rigour and inventiveness of these assessments, especially for senior appointments
- whether assessment processes include data on ethics and integrity
- whether employee records include information on ethical orientation
- whether whistleblowing policies encourage employees to report individuals with dubious ethics
- whether there are clear disciplinary and dismissal policies
- whether there are clear policies about communicating the reasons for disciplinary action or dismissal

The main output measure is the number of employees who have been asked to leave the company because of inappropriate ethics. In addition, a company might record the number of ethical breaches that appear to be the result of 'bad apples'. A company might also record the number of employees with ethical 'yellow cards', where there is some concern recorded on the employee's record. Also a company might record those departments that get low responses on ethical questions in the employee survey.

STEP 6: ASSURANCE: REDUCING THE RISK OF 'FOOLISH APPLES'

The main focus for reducing the risk of 'foolish apples' should be an identification of the situations where foolishness is likely to have significant consequences. For example, a company in a regulated industry might identify information presented to the regulator or accounting policies between regulated and unregulated businesses as critical areas. A branded consumer goods company might identify product quality. A retailer might identify the pricing of sale goods (think Tesco's strawberries). A university might identify research integrity. An exploration company might identify safety. Knowledge of past scandals in the industry and an understanding of where trust between the organisation and its stakeholders is most precious are helpful in identifying ethical risk areas.

These 'ethical risk' areas are different from, although may overlap with, areas where business choices can seriously damage performance, such as launches of new products, terms of major contracts or major investments. Ethical risk areas are less about money-at-risk and more about reputation-at-risk.

Once a risk area has been identified, input measures might include:

- whether codes of conduct exist tailored to these areas
- whether managers and employees in this area are given extra training, both to ensure their competence and to reinforce values, codes and the importance of ethical integrity
- whether managers and employees in this area have extra ethically related elements in their performance reviews
- whether rewards and incentives in this area are designed not to create inappropriate pressures or temptations
- whether special whistleblower policies are enacted for these areas
- whether special management attention, controls and approval processes exist in these areas
- whether special attention is given to audits and checks in these areas
- whether processes exist for reacting to, highlighting and learning from breaches

Output measures might include the number of occasions when audits, checks and controls have identified a problem, the number of whistleblower inputs, the number of incidents that were not prevented and the number of low scores on ethical questions in the employee survey from employees involved in this area.

STEP 7: ASSURANCE: REDUCING THE RISK OF 'PRESSURED APPLES'

The main focus for reducing the risk of 'pressured and tempted apples' is to identify situations where performance pressure or reward could cause managers or other employees to take short cuts. The booking of sales is clearly a tempting situation for sales people who are rewarded on sales volume. The recording of expenses is a tempting situation for employees who can reclaim expenses. Information submitted to the Bank of England about borrowing rates proved to be a tempting situation for managers whose bonuses and bank's reputation were affected by the data they were submitting. People can find it hard to be objective and act with integrity when their self-interest is at stake. As the saying goes, 'It is impossible to get someone to do something, when you are paying them not to do it'.

Often it is possible to put in controls or change incentives so as to eliminate the pressure or temptation. This is clearly the preferred solution. But, sometimes, eliminating the pressure or temptation is not possible. Where this is the case, both input measures and output measures can be similar to those for 'foolish apples'.

A systematic approach to setting the tone from the top, including a strategy for signalling to the organisation that the board is committed to high ethical standards, and for ensuring that the input and output measures are in place for the three sources of ethical risk – 'bad apples', 'foolish apples' and 'pressured apples' – should significantly reduce the ethical risk in most companies.

THE RESEARCH METHODOLOGY

The research examined the following questions:

a) What do boards do to provide an appropriate tone from the top?
b) How do boards monitor the tone that is being set and 'smell the air' in their companies?
c) How do non-executive directors check that their company has a good ethical compass?

Two hundred chairmen were invited to participate in the research. The response rate at circa 15 per cent was above expectations. From the end of July 2013 to late September 2013, interviews took place: mostly in person at the organisations' headquarters or by telephone. Throughout this report the term 'chairman' is used to denote the person chairing the organisation. While all respondents were men, the term encompasses chairmen and women. In one instance, the interview was with the group company secretary rather than the chairman.

The interviews lasted 30 minutes and covered questions on: board processes, board relationships, use of input and output measures, how boards test ethical standards, aspects of how the tone could be stronger and how boards have changed as a result of the increasing spotlight on the tone from the top.

While some questions were of a purely factual nature, others were more discussion based. Time was allowed for examples and opinions to be voiced, thereby providing context and colour to the more factual answers.

The responses were collated anonymously and analysed to identify patterns and trends.

THE QUESTIONNAIRE

Introduction – the purpose of research.

Confidentiality – all responses are confidential. No individual responses will be attributed.

A copy of the report will be sent to contributors.

1) Personal details of respondent (from company websites)

Name Job title Organisation Type of organisation	

2) How does your board provide ethical leadership to the organisation?

3) How does the board communicate the standards it would like the organisation to meet?

4) How do you ensure the board members 'walk the talk'? How is ethical leadership assessed in the board evaluation and individual director evaluations?

5) How do non-executive directors judge whether their company is putting enough effort into ethical leadership?

6) How does your board ensure it appoints executives who can give appropriate ethical leadership?

7) How do directors test/audit ethical standards lower down in the organisation?

8) How do you know whether your actions are working?

9) Which of the following input measures does your organisation use?

The company has a set of values	
The company has a code of conduct	
The company trains its people in the values	
The company trains its people in its code of conduct	
How many times would employees expect to be trained in their career at the company?	
Are employees evaluated for their ethics or adherence to the company values?	
Is there a whistleblowing policy?	
Is there a policy of doing an occasional ethics audit?	
Are there questions on ethics and values in the employee survey?	

10) Which of the following output measures does your organisation use?

Outcomes from employee surveys	
Individual manager targets from employee surveys	
% of managers with less than perfect ratings on ethics and values	
Number of ethical incidents	
Locations/countries/business units with ethical incidents	
Results from ethical audits	
Business turned away due to ethical concerns	

11) Is there one aspect of the tone from the top that could be stronger?

12) What feedback have external stakeholders given you?

13) Which action plans have been most successful and least successful? Why?

14) Has anything got in the way of implementing the actions identified?

15) How has your board changed due to the growing emphasis on the tone from the top?

16) What advice would you offer to other boards regarding the tone from the top?

17) What final advice would you offer the research project?

18) The report of research findings will be published in November this year. To which email address would you like it sent?

Thank you very much indeed for your participation in the research. This will remain strictly confidential with no individual comments or people identified. The only reference will be a list of participating organisations at the start of the report.

CASE STUDIES

Part II is a collection of case studies from experience in corporate life. They illustrate many of the aspects discovered from the research in Part I. Some case studies were experienced at first hand while others come from external organisations. These case studies illustrate the importance and value of the tone from the top from two perspectives: first, how getting it right mitigates ethical risk and enhances organisational performance; second, how one can learn from where things went wrong. The case studies show that time and again the 'how' as well as the 'what' of the tone from the top are hugely important. The signals sent by actions and behaviour can be just as influential as governance processes and decisions. Clearly all these aspects are needed, but many executives underestimate the impact of the behavioural signals they send. The case studies are from various levels in numerous organisations across several continents: from the board to the front line. Nevertheless, the influence of leadership's tone from the top can and should reach the furthest corners of the organisation.

To illustrate the point, a senior executive was reintroduced to an employee several years after their first meeting, which had taken place on the other side of the world. In the intervening years, the employee had been promoted several times. The senior executive asked her 'What was the secret of your success?' She replied that a fleeting conversation with a board member all those years ago had made an indelible mark and set a strong ethical compass that had served her well. In a different organisation, a senior female employee – but someone below the so-called glass ceiling – raised a highly sensitive commercial issue. It was an ethical dilemma. She had the courage to raise it because the chief executive had set an appropriate the tone from the top. After a nerve-racking investigation, in which she could have been turned upon as a disruptive whistleblower, changes were made. Subsequently she was offered a role above the so-called glass ceiling: as global head of compliance.

CASE STUDIES

The Vital Role of a Strong Board

Case Study 1 – Maintaining Board Strength

One chairman spoke of the way he manages board composition. This is a core area for him as he is thinking several years ahead. The start point is a review of strategy and markets. Following each refresh, there is a review of the likely skills and competencies needed at board level. These are drawn as a matrix showing an evolution over the time scale. There is then an overlay, showing each board member and their skills, experience and capabilities. That data is gathered from the annual board evaluation process as well as from the chairman's personal observation.

Reviewing current skills against future needs is still relatively rare at board level. However, the chairman organised the rotation of non-executive directors to create regular opportunities for bringing in new skills. Typically one non-executive director will retire or step down every year. Smooth phasing allows for regular planned change, unlike at some companies where radical change can bring in several non-executive directors at one time, storing up problems in future for their subsequent replacement – all at once. The chairman has established a tone from the top in which board composition is of paramount importance and he takes his responsibility for board strength very seriously.

Where the skills matrix shows gaps, it is clear what the next board recruit ought to have. Not only has this informed recruitment decisions relating to technical capability but also issues such as board diversity – in the broadest definition of the term.

Case Study 2 – Mediating Between Executive and Non-executive Directors

One comment that came from the research was that a dysfunctional board is toxic and possibly terminal for the organisation. This might sound melodramatic but chairmen gave examples of dysfunctionality, including in companies that no longer exist in their previous form. One organisation I came across years ago had a questionable structure in which an executive chairman worked alongside a chief executive. As both had executive leadership responsibilities, it was hardly surprising they did not see eye to eye on matters of strategy. Disagreements turned to more fundamental differences regarding who ran the company. It was alleged that both hired external PR agencies to fight it out in the press. The senior independent director allegedly stepped in and both leaders left rather suddenly.

Another company's board had differences of opinion on executive compensation. Emerging from a period of recession, the executive team was working very hard but felt the value and potential earnings from the long-term incentive plan were below the market. On the other hand, the non-executive directors felt that reward and potential earnings were already generous. They considered that the route to higher earnings was via performance, which at that time remained unproven.

External compensation consultants were engaged to investigate. Their conclusion was that against a comparator group of similar corporations, the potential value of the long-term incentive plan was below market. This was due to it being set at a smaller percentage of salary and had the maximum payout capped at a relatively low level. The problem was the growing difference of opinion between a group of executive directors who increasingly felt unfairly treated and a group of non-executive directors who felt the aspiration was unfounded. Context is helpful: most of the non-executive directors had decades of experience in fairly traditional industries. Their unstated sentiment was something like: 'How can they (the executives) be so greedy? Where I come from, a long-term incentive plan pays out possibly twice in your career.' By contrast, the unspoken sentiment of the executives was something like: 'How can they (the non-executives) be so mean? We are working insane hours for low potential reward so why should we try so hard?'

The solution was brokered by the chairman, senior independent director and HR head, who saw a way through to an outcome that would satisfy all parties. It was true that the quantum, or percentage of salary, was below market. In return for an increase in allocation, the performance conditions were changed to allow a higher maximum payout. This however was in return for a tightening of the performance conditions to make maximum payout much more challenging. Significant work was required to obtain shareholder agreement, with many individual shareholder meetings and much correspondence. But it was the chairman's clear tone from the top and leadership that drove a solution rather than pushing the problem away. Had he done that, it could have divided the board irreconcilably. Final proposals were drawn up, voted on and approved at the company's annual general meeting. Satisfaction was restored because the executives felt real opportunity had been restored and the non-executives felt that if ever there were to be a maximum payout, the executives probably would have earned every cent of it. The chairman's leadership in grappling with a problem that would not go away had combined with resolute adherence to strong governance from the senior independent director. Once persuaded, he led the discussions with shareholders and came under considerable personal pressure. He ran a robust process and addressed the shareholders' concerns, with meticulous attention to detail. This paid off. When it came to the vote, a substantial majority were in favour and the motion was carried. This sent clear signals regarding governance, process, appropriateness and behaviour.

Strong Governance is a Pre-requisite

Case Study 3 – Reward Governance

Many companies suffer from perceptions and even the reality of reward being unfair or too opaque. One addressed the problem not just by training all managers on the reward tools they should use, but how they should balance decisions, taking into account performance, the differentiation of performance, internal and external market factors, retention and individual market worth. That was then put into the context of the available budget and the employer's ability to pay.

But what stood out was the governance and transparency applied to the pay review process. Once initial proposals had been received, a moderation process was used to check on managers 'under-cooking' or 'over-cooking' their proposals. A key concern was to ensure fair application of process even though it yielded different outcomes owing to the differentiation of performance. At the time, no data was collected on LGBT employees but it probably would be today. Once complete, there were reviews to check whether any bias had been evident relating to age, gender, disability or length of service. Another piece of analysis examined whether managers had been awarded a different percentage increase compared with non-managers. A policy statement confirmed that directors would not be awarded more than the average for the workforce, as their pay was strongly incentive based. Internal audit were willingly asked to undertake a full review of the process, including more than just checks on the payroll to look for duplicate and phantom employees. Finally, checks were put in place to ensure that pay drift outside the pay review process were in place throughout the year.

All these factors were investigated and the results were published in aggregate to the whole workforce. Employees applauded the transparency and care in the process. They felt the company was trying to 'do the right thing'. The tone from the top demonstrated strong governance and a commitment to showing its value. The additional benefit was that with the process laid bare, few employees raised concerns about the outcome. Had any employees or managers felt tempted to abuse of even defraud the system, there were clear messages regarding the independent audit and scrutiny of the process from end to end. Throughout the exercise, leadership's behaviour demonstrated a commitment to fairness.

Case Study 4 – The Need for Unwavering Resolve Once a Decision is Made

A multinational was conducting an operational review in a subsidiary considered to be a 'difficult' region. The country concerned has a low per capita GDP and its capital city is a dangerous place. The country CEO was a local national who had been sponsored by a member of the main board. From an emotional point of view, the local CEO was 'his man'. However, at the operational review, it became increasingly apparent that the business would not make its numbers that year. When challenged by the chairman, the local CEO exuded confidence, saying 'it will be a walk in the park'. However, presentations by other local executives, especially the CFO, revealed a more challenged picture.

Separately, concerns had been raised about leadership in the local company and the way people had been brought in and exited. There were concerns about ethics and something of a fear culture. The main board member concerned was advised but had some difficulty in accepting the need for a change of leadership. As evidence mounted, an investigation was commissioned. It was a delicate subject because the local CEO was a person of colour, a local figure and had enjoyed air cover from the main board director. The board therefore insisted on thorough, impartial research. The investigation substantiated the need for change and a plan was drawn up. It was complex, involving succession by bringing in a new CEO – a foreign national from the other side of the world – and synchronising local stock exchange announcements. Regulators on both sides of the world would need to be informed.

The main board reached a clear decision based on objective performance data. It also understood the need for change based on the wider cultural and management climate data. It was therefore appropriate to act and be seen to be acting swiftly and effectively.

The change project was managed from the head office. Local lawyers in the country of operation were engaged. Many details were covered, ranging from briefing the local chairman and regional CEO to minute-by-minute communications plans, to confidentially obtaining a work permit for the successor.

Owing to the geographical dispersion of the people involved, numerous audio and video-conferences spanned multiple time zones. Announcements were drafted and redrafted then aligned thematically. The HR head flew to the local business and was greeted by an armed protection officer in the arrivals hall. The hotel had razor wire around the perimeter and meetings with the local lawyers were under cover. Two days before the appointed moment of change, the local CEO suspected that something was happening. His local intelligence found out that certain people were heading for – or were already in – the country. The local Chairman started to 'wobble'. Being a no-nonsense, straight-talking type, he said 'why don't we just accelerate and deal with it right now?' That risked unravelling all kind of communications – to the stock exchange, the press, employees, the wider business, customers and suppliers. Much persuasion was required, however clear guidance was provided by the main board director who said 'We stick to the plan. We execute the plan'. Having said this several times, the stress was contained and people got back to the job in hand.

This leadership was essential to stop the plan unravelling, which could have been a compliance and reputational disaster. It was one of those times where a very clear tone from the top was essential. The main board director showed great executive presence through:

- gravitas – how he acted, remaining calm under pressure
- his choice of words – and how they were spoken, and
- how he looked – confident and assured, even via video-conferencing.

These three behavioural elements combined to show strong leadership in the face of erratic emotion that was injecting unpredictability and uncertainty into a highly charged, stressful situation. The tone from the top stopped the whole plan from unravelling.

The plan was executed as planned. Multiple announcements were synchronised and issued. Executives followed their brief and the successor took up office two hours after the outgoing executive was told the decision. Press reporting was generally favourable and the organisation was stabilised quickly as the new leader toured the operations and major customers to establish himself.

The way the outgoing leader was treated also sent signals to the organisation. While the decision was implemented swiftly, dialogue continued with the individual for a sufficient period of time afterwards.

In this case study, the board was acting in a clear decisive manner but also ensuring that its decision was implemented in an exemplary way. The board took a broad view of both objective performance and subjective input to conduct a fact-finding investigation before acting. Having taken action, care was taken to position appropriately, the messaging and signalling to both internal and external audiences. But the clear strategy nearly came to nothing. It was the behavioural leadership, the tone from the top, that held it together.

Special Attention to Ethics is Increasing

Case Study 5 – Linking Incentive Plan Membership to the Ethics Code

A new incentive plan was being rolled out to operating companies. It was significantly different by treating subsidiaries as if they were owned by private equity. With 'notional debt' to pay back to the parent, the race was on to drive up revenue, margin, cash conversion and service. It was also important to reduce sales general and administrative costs, customer defections and working capital. The plan applied to senior executives but they could not achieve the objectives without huge support from local management teams.

The CEO therefore updated local business unit incentive plans. In return for enhanced opportunities for reward, membership of local plans required a physical signature on the company code of conduct (that is ethics code). The plan rules clearly stated that membership was by written individual invitation. For membership to be confirmed, participants had to sign a declaration on the code of conduct that they would abide by it and would pursue all business goals with ethics and integrity. Further, they would conduct themselves ethically and with the highest integrity. They were asked to fax or scan a signed copy of the code to the head office, for it to be held centrally. Payments would only be made having confirmed that each plan member's signature on the code of conduct had been held for the duration of the plan.

Perhaps somewhat ahead of his time, the CEO also changed the incentive plan rules to include clauses on claw-back and malus. Claw back is where incentive pay can be withheld or repaid by the employee in the event of results mis-statement, errors, computational errors or other technical reasons. Claw-back could also happen if the way in which an incentive was earned was contrary to company policy, the code of conduct or good business ethics. Malus is where incentive pay can be withheld or clawed back not because of a technical reason within the plan, but because of inappropriate conduct by the plan member. If, for example, a manager was technically eligible for a large incentive payment but was nearing the end of a disciplinary process for improper conduct, the employer reserved the right to withhold payment in the event of him or her being found guilty.

The signal sent by getting plan members to sign a declaration as a pre-requisite for membership caused people to stop and think. When regular incentive plan updates were issued, they always referred to the pursuit of business success by ethical means. This acted as a reminder should any 'bad apples', 'foolish apples' or 'tempted apples' have thought about doing business in other ways.

Case Study 6 – Identifying Great Managers, a Spotlight on Excellence, Knowledge Transfer

A highly distributed multinational faced a number of commercial, competitive and cultural challenges. Former exclusive licences were gone and the competitive intensity was increasing rapidly. New players had entered the market and were prepared to make a big statement with substantial capital investment. The multinational's businesses included small countries and major metropolitan areas. They operated in very different markets and cultures. To illustrate the point, within the portfolio were businesses operating in countries with some of the lowest and the very highest per capita GDP in the world.

One leadership challenge was to address ethics and performance in a way that brought the business units closer together. This unifying theme was central to enabling the businesses to up their game and learn more from each other. A cultural change programme was adopted and sponsored by the CEO. The aim was to establish a new tone from the top, focused on three things: great financial performance, great people management and great customer experience. Its central plank was an employee engagement tool. It consisted of a short on-line questionnaire with all employees asked to rate each one on a five-point scale (1–5). The scale ranged from 'I strongly disagree' (1), to 'I strongly agree' (5). However, provided response rates were high, the tool enabled all managers to have a personal scorecard. It was therefore used to identify who were the great managers and who were inadequate managers. It was essential to have very high participation rates. Strict confidentiality controls were put in place so as not to identify individual respondents.

The questions addressed a range of topics, several of which covered the ethics of how people were managed, recognised, developed and how poor performance was dealt with. As a result, it became clear who were the managers with the most engaged employees – the people most likely to give discretionary extra effort, to address issues and to take performance seriously. And that meant treating under-performance, in all its guises, seriously and dealing with it.

The CEO would travel the world to review the operations. Each operational review would have a set agenda that included environment, health and safety, operating performance, financial measures, investment, service and people measures and issues. It would also include items on talent and succession. Once the engagement results were available, the agendas of operational reviews were changed. The first two hours of any business visit included a meeting with the top scoring managers of that business. Interestingly, the top scoring managers came from all levels of the company. In some cases it was the first time that managers from such diverse areas had attended the same meeting. It was certainly unusual for them to meet the CEO. The agenda was to congratulate them, to acknowledge them, to listen to what they did to manage their people well and to note how best to transfer knowledge and experience to other businesses.

In particular, questions were asked about what kind of ethical problems were faced and how they had been addressed. By focusing on everyday examples of how supervisors and managers went about their jobs, a rich understanding was acquired. This was used to signal the importance of ethics and to educate others around the world. It set an example and changed the focus of the whole organisation from simply 'numbers, numbers, numbers' to a much more holistic view of management, financial performance, people performance, discretionary extra effort and recognition. I will refer to this process in more detail in Part III. The tone from the top showed that simply delivering your numbers was no longer enough. It was now a much broader issue and it included behaviour as well as decisions.

The process was run every six months to a relentless drumbeat of survey, results, action and follow-up. Each manager had a personal scorecard. Following that, each manager was set individual targets for what was expected at the next survey. Managers were required to hold focus group sessions with their teams to ask what they should do differently to improve their score next time. Departments worked together on how collective improvements could be made. This may sound simple, but the actions required for a top score are complex, systemic and pervasive as we will see in Part III. The first time the survey was run, managers were told that their scorecards were for calibration purposes. With each successive wave of running the survey, the requirement tightened because a persistently under-scoring manager isn't really a manager. This has profound implications for any organisation that wants to pursue this way of managing. There was a clear tone from the top that it was a whole-company programme and not a passing HR initiative. After all, it was sponsored by the CEO. As management actions changed, each wave of the survey produced a league table of businesses ranked according to their engagement score. The league table became the single most accurate predictor of financial performance in the company.

There is Growing Awareness of the Implications of Signalling

Case Study 7 – Consulting Employees Through a Takeover

This case study was originally published by the UK's CIPD – The Chartered Institute of Personnel and Development. It is freely available from the CIPD website: http://www. cipd.co.uk/publicpolicy/policy-reports/consulting-employees-charter-international. aspx. When a business is transferred, UK TUPE (Transfer of Undertakings Protection of Employment) regulations generally require employers to consult employee representatives. Where an acquisition is effected by a transfer of shares, TUPE does not apply because the employer's identity does not change. However, this doesn't mean the employer can simply do what they like. Changes to the rules on UK takeovers in 2012 required employers to consult with employees and provide answers to questions raised: the changes were in the aftermath of Kraft's takeover of Cadbury. In that situation, the view that persists in the public memory is simple: Kraft promised time and again that on acquiring Cadbury they would not close a particular factory in Wales. A few days after acquiring the confectioner, they closed the factory in Wales. This provoked an outcry and questions were raised in Parliament. The law was change.

Charter International plc was the ultimate owner of two international engineering businesses: ESAB, which is a world leader in welding, cutting and automation, and Howden, an applications engineering business for air and gas handling equipment mainly in the energy sector. At the time of the takeover, Charter employed 12,500 people across 122 countries. More than 20 languages were used in the company. Its CEO had been replaced following a profit warning and the company received two takeover offers. A £1.5 billion offer from US-based Colfax Corporation was subsequently recommended by the Charter board and completed in 2013. It was the largest corporate transaction on the London Stock Exchange that year.

Charter's HR Director and board appreciated the value of signalling to the global workforce. The new regulations weren't just an opportunity to demonstrate compliance; they enabled the board to give employees a voice in meaningful ways. This was deemed essential for reputation management, to assist wide-ranging efforts to improve overall performance and to maintain employee engagement through a high-stress period. By showing commitment to proper process, due diligence and strict governance, the board's aim was to send clear signals about professionalism, performance and the potential benefit for all. The CEO addressed many employee meetings and said:

> *You may not be able to change the ultimate outcome of what's going on, but consider this: We have two choices: we can either look out of the window quaking in our boots not knowing what to do for six months OR we can redouble our efforts to make this the very best company we can. If we sit here doing nothing, the new owners will draw their own conclusions regarding who is effective and a worse company will mean more restructuring. If we do all we can to improve the company, maybe the new owners wil say "wow, that's a group of switched-on people. Looks like we need to keep them".*

To obtain employee opinions, a UK-listed company being taken over needs to consult employee representatives. Charter was the first required to consult its people under the new rules. In the absence of any details guidance in the rules or from the Takeover Panel, Charter had to design its own consultation mechanism. This presented significant challenges, given the widespread geographical operations and the very short timescale to complete the task.

In late summer 2011, potentially two offers could have been forthcoming for Charter. While only one formal offer was made, the purpose of the consultation was to enable employees to comment on one or more offers versus staying independent.

Global HR leaders were informed of the consultation process by audio conference and the normal 'cascade' briefing process. A clear signalling opportunity was that while the conference calls were led by the HR Director, the CEO, CFO and General Counsel and Group Company Secretary were in his office as he led the calls. The senior executives were introduced as participants to show support for the key role local HR would need to play in the consultation. The 42-page Colfax offer was circulated to HR, employee representatives and trade unions, and in some cases local focus groups, for them to read and take advice. Translation was done locally. Headquarters HR designed a feedback form which included all sections of the proposal and invited comments using a 1–5 scale (1 = strongly disagree; 2 = disagree; 3 = no comment; 4 = agree; 5 = strongly agree). There was also a 250-word section for free-format comments. The mix of numerical and free-format responses enabled strength and depth of feeling to be captured by business and by geography.

The consultation period elicited more than 100 sets of responses from Charter entities and ran for just one month from start to finish. Throughout, the HR function led global conference calls, which continued to be attended by Charter and ESAB CEOs and the General Counsel, who confirmed the process. The participants were local managing directors and regional HR heads. Involvement of the whole senior leadership team was seen as critical to raising the profile of the consultation process and ensuring a good response. Responses were subsequently consolidated at head office and incorporated into a spread sheet. All verbatim comments were collated – unedited – into a nine-page document. Leadership believed it was important to include unabridged comments as a means of validating the draft summary position.

To reassure the Takeover Panel that the opinion accurately represented the views of the workforce, a sub-committee of representatives was set up, one from each region or line of business. As a result of their feedback, some adjustments were made to the draft opinion, which was subsequently posted on the internal company intranet and circulated to all employees worldwide.

The opinion was broadly supportive of the proposed takeover. However, a number of concerns were raised about the possible impact of the takeover on specific business areas. The opinion noted that Colfax had given assurances that Charter employers 'would continue to comply with the contractual and other entitlements in relation to pension and employment rights of existing employees', but that the company had not supplied any information about the potential impact on employment. Accordingly, the opinion listed a number of specific questions, for example:

- Will one or other of the companies be sold?
- Will pension schemes be fully funded?
- Will existing union agreements be honoured?

Reinforcing the consultation by its existing cascade processes and 'town hall' meetings to explain the wider background and correct some misunderstandings, Charter was able to send the final opinion to Colfax in time for them to respond to employee concerns in their shareholder circular. This in turn was made available to Charter employees via the Charter website. In this way, the feedback process enabled Charter employees to see that Colfax had taken note of their comments.

The consultation process reinforced the relationship between the company, its leadership and its employees. The company had sent letters to employees who would be among early leavers, confirming that promises and policies would be honoured. Colfax said they would honour not just the law, but company policy and practice for at least a year – which they did for a longer period. The letters effectively said to employees, 'Here is the deal'. Most of the fears employees had about the risk to their pensions were removed. Employees were grateful that the company had given no steer on how they should respond to the consultation and appreciated the fair representation of their views. Shareholders were also given some reassurance – in a kind of 'reverse due diligence' – that the companies were behaving with integrity and transparency and that there was a reduced risk of the kind of public criticism that followed the Kraft takeover of Cadbury.

Technically, the consultation process represented a significant achievement for the company. The scale of the exercise was unprecedented, involving subsidiaries across the world from South America to China, Russia to South Africa. The severe timing constraints were overcome partly by focusing the process on the specific issues on which an employee response was required. In some respects, management had to adopt an *ad hoc* approach, using a mix of communications and consultation methods and driving the process centrally while ensuring employee views were faithfully reflected. Transparency was uppermost in leadership's mind and needed a consistent and intensive effort, including repeated references back to local businesses for confirmation that messages had been properly understood and recorded.

There are lessons too about how to achieve an effective employee 'voice'. Employees were motivated to contribute to the process, both because they had a critical interest in the outcome and because they saw a real opportunity to influence the outcome. It was clearly not possible to rule out the prospect of redundancies following the takeover. Nevertheless, the consultation exercise ensured people issues had a place on the agenda when shareholders were considering the Colfax proposal. It was clear that employee interests were taken into account. The consultation was also seen to be instrumental in maintaining morale and reducing the likelihood of good people jumping ship in the short term.

The consultation requirement in the Takeover Code was included essentially to reduce the likelihood of a recurrence of the Kraft/Cadbury experience, which undermined employee relations and was widely perceived as a reputational and public relations disaster for Kraft. The consultation requirement reinforces the importance of companies being seen to behave ethically and responsibly, sending continuous signals to multiple audiences that they are 'doing the right thing'. Charter's annual report underlined its commitment to corporate responsibility in areas such as health and safety, management training, ethics training, anti-bribery and corruption and employee relations. The company saw this as a source of competitive edge. Its employee communication and consultation processes were an integral part of this wider business agenda.

Coherence of signalling also enabled a focus on performance improvement through the takeover process. Leadership identified a working capital problem in one subsidiary. Explaining the opportunity to managers, the Executive Committee said a significant and sustained reduction on working capital would be in everyone's interests: shareholders, the acquirer and managers. Against the background of involvement, managers appreciated the value of their role in improving operations. A working capital reduction incentive plan was designed, approved and communicated to key managers. Inclusion was by personal written invitation from the CEO. Clear targets were specified and proper governance processes implemented. Participants were reminded of the option of 'do nothing and the new owners will form one view' or 'drive for the best company we can deliver and they will form a very different view'.

Over a six-month period, a resolute focus on debtors, cash collection, inventory size, inventory turn, SG&A costs, payment terms, slow moving stock, product range simplification and many other aspects yielded tens of millions of pounds. This was real money in the bank, not some form of accounting trick. As a result, when the third quarter financial results were published in late 2011, they pleasantly surprised the markets. One press commentator said: 'Maybe Charter could have stayed independent after all.' But by this time the takeover was proceeding apace. In response to improved financial performance, Colfax's shareholders concluded that the proposed takeover might be acquiring a better company than they at first had thought. Not surprisingly, investors bought more Colfax shares. The offer for Charter was a mix of cash and Colfax shares. As the Colfax share price rose towards $30, the value of the offer increased. At the time of the deal closing, the value of the takeover was several hundred million pounds more than the initial indicative offer. All employees who were shareholders benefited from this.

Leadership's signalling across many channels – consistently and persistently – set a clear tone from the top in what was a very stressful situation. By behaving with integrity, and being seen to behave ethically, employee concerns were surfaced, given voice, responded to and resolved. The need to drive performance was communicated and behavioural signals from the top showed an intense unbending work ethic. The working capital reduction programme rewarded those who delivered the results and more widely improved the value of the takeover, thereby rewarding all employees who were shareholders.

Case Study 8 – The Implications of Signalling

An American CEO was regarded as a great communicator, something of a Ronald Regan of the corporate world. His short, pithy one-liners resonated with audiences because of the simplicity of his message. In particular, junior employees around the world admired the clarity of thought and were left in no doubt about what the CEO stood for. While some senior people would find fault in what they perceived to be over-simplification and a denial of market dynamics, nonetheless the messages were clear. They signalled what was expected, how things should be done but, above all, the velocity that was now required. There was a very clear tone from the top – it was about performance. The CEO also sponsored a new ethics code and so the tone was more than simply 'give me better numbers'. The ethics code spoke of straight talking with honesty and integrity, preserving human dignity, even, for example, when dismissing people. But he was clear on the signalling power of removing non-performers and those whose behaviour undermined performance. He said: 'For the right reasons, one sacking is worth a thousand memos.'

Several years before the arrival of the CEO, a subsidiary had experienced rapid growth and was the darling of the markets. With success came hubris for some. One executive who had a commanding role in technology had started to exhibit bad behaviour. He would show contempt for certain people mentioned in meetings. He played increasingly to his agenda. Employees started to feel manipulated. As is so often the case, there was no single outrageous blunder but a steadily growing list of inappropriate comments, cultural and ethical misdemeanours.

A manager was having a business conversation with the executive. At the end of the conversation the manager was asked to fix a problem in the lavatories. When told the helpline number for Facilities, the executive's behaviour clearly indicated an expectation of the manager making the call. The executive installed some unapproved software on his computer. It produced sound effects from Star Trek, annoying people who came into his office and the person in the adjacent office. A female employee lodged a complaint about the way the executive had peeled a banana in front of her. She alleged it was full of sexual innuendo. And so the list evolved. The executive's behaviour was highlighted to top management who noted it and asked the informants to understand that the matter was in hand and that action would be taken. For their own protection, they should not address the individual head-on.

Centrally, a review of expenses claims was undertaken. This was an annual exercise as part of good governance – to see a league table of all expense claimants in descending order of total amount. Naturally, at the top of the list, came those employees who had been relocated at the company's expense. Moving house is not a low-cost expense claim. Further down the list was the executive. While his total claims were not for excessive amounts, some of the categories were, to say the least, unusual. Two items stood out as not being business expenditure. One was a horsewhip, the other a camera.

The final straw followed fairly quickly. At a company retreat for senior executives, delegates were enjoying pre-dinner drinks. The arrangements had been confirmed as 'cash bar'. The executive, however, bought a round of drinks and asked for a receipt. A colleague asked why he had asked for one. Allegedly, the reply was a dismissive, surly tone indicating contempt. It was clear that the bill would be charged to the company. However, everything had been seen by the CEO who had instructed that it was a cash bar. He later said that when he buys someone a drink, it is a gift from him and not from the company.

The executive's employment was terminated. The fact became known across a wide audience very quickly. The message was received as reassurance that there are ethical people who will do the right thing. There was a great collective sigh of relief. But there was more than that. There was a strong sense of comfort that the heart of the organisation was in the right place and bad behaviour would not be tolerated. In the aftermath of the decision and the finer points of the exit, the executive was asked to sign a declaration that he had returned all company equipment. It turned out that he had a substantial file server at home. This complex piece of technology had come with a huge price tag, paid for by the company. A van was sent to collect it. This also became known and the folklore of the organisation acquired a new 'war story'.

The American CEO was right. Numerous memos could have been written, asserting the right of the employer to protect its assets. No end of memos could have been written reminding employees about how to get facilities problems fixed or what is acceptable within the expenses policy. No doubt guidance on the harassment policy could have explained that harassment occurs when the recipient understands actions or behaviour to be intimidating, demeaning or insulting. And so it could have gone on – but to little effect. The firing of the executive sent a clear signal that the employer would not tolerate such behaviour.

Years later, at a different company's executive retreat, a group of senior people were checking out at the hotel. One director was at the front of the queue but was somewhat preoccupied with his incoming email to his hand-held device. The hotel receptionist asked whether he had used the mini-bar. He replied yes, he had drunk some mineral water. She therefore added it to the bill. He interjected, saying that he would like one bill for the room and would settle the mini-bar personally in cash. He was completely unaware of any queue behind him or that it included other members of the company. But they noticed his action, which sent a signal of ethical behaviour. It has been said by several commentators that an ethical company 'does the right thing even when they know no one is looking'. It was clear that this director was unaware of who was in the checkout queue three people further back. But the story of him doing the right thing became known – not as an unusual practice, but as someone simply doing the right thing.

Case Study 9 – Use of Language and the Signals It Sends

A CEO used strong language. However, under stress, his use of bad language increased. Among director colleagues, this could be contained because it was understood in context. That said, there are always limits beyond which intervention is required. As pressure mounted, his swearing was no longer confined to small meetings of senior people. At larger meetings, attended by divisional heads, the use of such language sent a signal that 'it is OK to use bad language'.

Senior leaders rarely appreciate the impact and influence their behaviour has on people lower down an organisation – a topic to which we will return later. Human nature is to look after one's self-interest and so adopting the behaviour patterns of one's boss or of senior people is much more common than one might think. For example, in another company, a new CEO with a ruthless reputation had a striking shaved head. In presentations and 'town hall' meetings he adopted a certain swagger. Within three months, the haircuts of his senior team (comprising mostly quite young men) became more and more severe. Their demeanour when presenting took on a certain hubris. Slowly but surely, and maybe inadvertently, they were copying their boss.

Once a signal has been sent several times, people pick up on it and start to emulate the behaviour. And so it was with the CEO who swore. One or two divisional heads started swearing too and no doubt their people started to copy them. Intervention was required because within this 'trickle-down effect' there was real danger of disengagement, as well as claims of harassment, bullying and other forms of discrimination. Employees would be right to make such claims. Where behaviour causes offence or is received in an intimidating way, that is where the misdemeanour takes place.

An eminent law firm was engaged to provide guidance and training to the executive committee, including the CEO. The firm is regarded as a leading litigation house and has handled some high-profile cases. In one such case, a trader in the financial services sector had resigned following foul language from his manager. This was not a one-off event. The language was not generic either. It had been highly offensive and very directed at the trader. The trader sued the employer. At the court case, the manager said: 'What do you expect? – This is a trading floor and that means the use of industrial language. That's what we do here.' The judge wanted to understand whether the manager's foul language was an exclamation, that is, not directed at another person. For example, if you accidentally hit your thumb with a hammer, you will probably swear, but it is not intended to be offensive to another person. It became apparent that the bad language was no such exclamation. It was persistent and fully focused on the trader. Such was the anger of the manager that he was also using repeated pointing gestures while swearing. The trader resigned on ill health grounds and had trouble finding another job. It was clear that the manager's use of bad language had got out of control and had accelerated as it became more personally focused. The judge ordered compensation and loss of earnings of well in excess of a million dollars.

The law firm therefore had great credentials to advise and train the senior team at the company whose CEO was swearing a little too much. The training event was arranged. The trainer appeared very unassuming as he introduced himself. Little did his audience know that he was the chief litigator who had won the trader's settlement. Walking to the flip chart, he said: 'Let's put some examples of behaviour on the chart. At the top means reprehensible; an absolute no-no, whereas the bottom of the page means ok, we can live with that.' He continued: 'Ok, so where would you put: sexual assault in the workplace?' The audience said 'At the top.' The trainer said: 'And where would you put use of the word "Shit" in the context of someone realising they had made a mistake?' 'At the bottom,' replied the audience. As you can imagine, what followed was a series of ethical dilemmas regarding context, use of language, intention, the way language is received by different people including people of colour, minorities and

LGBT employees. The audience learned that what on paper looks identical can have very different meaning according to context, the way it is said and where or to whom such language is directed. This was the 'Ah-ha' moment. The audience realised that their frame of reference could not be the same as others' and there was risk in using inappropriate language.

This largely solved the problem. Interestingly, as soon as the leader stopped using certain words, the people lower down the organisation stopped as well. Such is the power of behavioural signals. This is an example of where the tone from the top has profound impact. One could argue that it is the very essence of the tone from the top – the tone of language and its impact on others. That impact has a multiplier effect as it influences successive levels of organisations. If you have any doubts, try this experiment: introduce a novel new way of expressing something topical in your organisation. Choose a word or phrase not currently part of the organisation's vocabulary. Then see how it takes hold, eventually coming back to you from others. Soon it will be copied and used more extensively than you might have imagined.

Different Approaches May Be Relevant According to a Company's Stage of Development

Case Study 10 – The Need for Consistency in the Face of a Failed IPO

An independent energy company was heading for an initial public offering. Great effort went into growing the business, acquiring new licences and improving operational efficiency. In the early stages of the company, high capital intensity meant that with a relatively small workforce, salaries, structures and people-related costs were a small fraction of overall operating costs. The tone from the top was therefore one of 'get it done and build a track record of safety and compliance'. Senior team cohesion was strong; everyone shared a common goal and they all looked forward to realising their share of investment.

Then a combination of adverse factors created head winds. Output was not as high as planned, one asset started underperforming significantly, a series of production problems delayed deliveries and expected new business did not materialise. Pressure mounted and there were some personnel changes within the team. Differences of opinion began to surface. Operations felt that operating the assets mandated an organisation with the infrastructure to deliver. The commercial functions felt that licences and operating assets could be acquired and then sold on, with the company taking a slice of the action from what was ultimately delivered. That would mandate a very small organisation of different capabilities. The external economic climate and certainly the appetite for IPOs worsened in the recession following the 2009 financial crisis. As investors became increasingly risk averse, it became clear that the IPO was not going to happen.

For a time, differences of approach were contained to the top team. However as managers joined various senior meetings, they saw at first hand that the senior team was less of a team than before. The tone from the top had become less clear. Now it was a combination of performance and politics with a growing uncertainty about the future. External facilitation helped senior management to clarify the operating model and the organisation structure. Some behavioural issues were also addressed. A communications plan was drawn up and a new focus was set for the way the top team would interact with wider management. There was a growing realisation of the need for consistent signalling, especially in the face of changing commercial, financial and wider economic conditions.

With greater clarity and a new resolve, management focused on addressing the technical issues and on improving performance. The tone from the top was more supportive. The run of bad luck came to an end and a few months later new opportunities were identified and a sense of progress re-established. The learning was that sending consistent signals in the face of business difficulty enabled the company to stay focused. Taking noise out of the system, especially at senior levels, was an important factor in stabilising and refocusing the organisation. Above all, it was leadership's behaviour that sent those signals.

Case Study 11 – The Need for Values that Allow a Change of Direction

A small technology company had prided itself on fast, entrepreneurial action. The tone from the top could be summarised as 'speed, agility and delivery'. Growth was fast, based on a technology advantage. The behaviour of company leaders sent confident signals of a bright future stretching to the horizon. However, as further new technologies came to market, the technology advantage was eroded and the company was left with excessive debt and declining revenue. Eventually a radical change programme was approved but it came as a shock to the workforce who had difficulty aligning the original tone from the top with the new reality. With hindsight, senior management felt that the inevitable volatility of being a start-up did not enable the organisation to commit too strongly to a set of values that could become incompatible with commercial reality.

Case Study 12 – Dealing with Disruptors in a Post-merger Integration

For a much larger technology company, consolidation of the industry meant acquisitions. A mature and long-established operator was acquiring a new entrant. The message to shareholders was: 'We are buying the new entrant for its management team.' An interesting nuance was that several of the new entrant's management had been poached from the mature operator. In some ways it was a case of déjà vu. The CEO of the new entrant was appointed CEO of the merged entity.

It is often said that there is no such thing as a merger. There are always winners and losers and the way to tell which company is taking over the other, is to look at the management structure six months after the deal closes and note the origin of those in-post. In this case, there were mixed messages and the tone from the top was inconsistent.

People in the smaller new entrant felt they had a ticket to ride in the new merged entity. It was like going from being a big fish in a small pond to being a big fish in a very big pond. On the other hand, people in the larger company felt that they were paying hundreds of millions to buy the new entrant, so they had every right to call the shots. They displayed just a little arrogance as if to say 'I am the parent and you are the child' towards people in the acquired company. Conversely, the newly acquired relied on the external message that they had been bought for their management skill. Further, as their man was now running the show, it was clear who should prevail.

At divisional level and across one function, in particular, the head was determined to demonstrate the use of fair process when appointing people to the newly redesigned structure. There was a great deal of transitional work to be done and those not appointed were offered a fixed term continuation of employment before redundancy would take effect. This, of course, assumed that people would continue to work professionally, putting the needs of the organisation above any personal agenda. However, human nature being what it is meant that tribal rivalries were kept well and truly alive. While some went underground, others remained visible. These manifested themselves in different ways. Some instructions were ignored. Others implemented decisions to a different set of criteria or said one thing but did another. Some joint teams were set up to resolve certain business issues. Despite clearly nominated leaders, rivalries within some of the teams meant challenge and insufficient progress. In some areas, fundamental differences of approach led to dysfunctionality within integration teams. Leadership had not signalled how to address the issue of both parties thinking they were the victors. The tone from the top was in effect two tones from two tops.

The divisional head therefore had to set their own tone from the top, based on high integrity and fair process. Clear standards were laid out. Governance was tightened and senior oversight of decisions, particularly on appointments, was implemented. Timescales for project completion were tightened to drive a sense of urgency that required collaboration. Disruptors were identified and warned individually about what was expected from them. Where disruption persisted, it was clear what the impact was on the tightened project delivery dates. Taking a factual approach, the divisional head set about removing those who remained unwilling to put the interests of the organisation first. This sent clear signals about expectations and performance but, above all, about cooperation and team working. The new culture was established and as the organisation settled, a new tone from the top clarified the standards required.

Reducing the Number of 'Bad Apples'

Case Study 13 – Removing a Divisional Head to Allow Staff to Flourish

A senior business leader was responsible for a group of divisional functions. Some were led by a divisional manager who reported to the business leader. Let's call the two people the leader and the manager. The manager had undoubted technical skill but dysfunctional leadership capability. The leader had tried various ways of improving the manager's performance, with particular emphasis on how he managed his people. At one point, the manager was assigned an external coach to give behavioural guidance. But this was not successful. The leader remained reluctant to take action because of the excellent depth of specialist knowledge held by the manager. He felt that the manager's unique technical know-how and historic knowledge made him a deep source of 'company memory'. Employees in service functions found the manager very difficult to work with. Employee turnover among key people reporting to the manager was rising. There was discontent and product deadlines were not being met. Through a process of Socratic questioning and coaching the leader, it became clear that the manager should be replaced. The leader remained reluctant but was eventually persuaded.

A change plan was drawn up, including succession, appropriate briefings of all the stakeholders as well as handling the termination event with sensitivity. On the appointed day, a minute-by-minute timetable of events was executed and the change implemented. Local trade unions were briefed just ahead of the rest of the workforce. There was clear relief when the successor was announced and employees were thankful for the way the change had been managed. Under the new management, talent started to come forward, new ideas were offered and overall effectiveness increased. Communication and collaboration improved. People rose to new challenges and were recognised for their contribution. Several issues came to light after the manager's departure that led the leader to appreciate that his reluctance to make the change was not right.

Over many years, directors have said to me that they 'never fired anyone too soon'. By that, they mean they always gave people the benefit of the doubt for too long. It is easy to be wise after the event, but often where behaviour is dysfunctional no amount of technical expertise can surmount the organisational and motivational problems it brings. The impact on productivity and engagement in this example spanned multiple departments, even countries. Delays cost the organisation market share.

In this case study, the tone from the top evolved through a series of stages. Employee perception was at first neutral as the perception was 'This is a local issue for local management to resolve'. Then the tone was perceived negatively, with an increasing number of employees thinking and saying 'Why isn't anyone listening to us?' When the change was implemented, the level of planning and preparation became clear and the perception changed again to 'Thank you, you have listened and taken action'.

However there was a missed opportunity. Had action been taken sooner, it could have set a clearer and more consistent tone from the top. That could have been one of 'We will not tolerate poor behaviour, no matter how technically capable someone may be'. And the action would have conveyed the message louder than any announcement or presentation.

Reducing the Number of 'Foolish Apples'

Case Study 14 – Changing the Agenda Changes the Culture

This case study comes from a simple directive from a CEO who was determined to take his company's Environment, Health and Safety performance from rather pedestrian to knocking on the door of world-class performance.

A new requirement was communicated to every manager across the global operations. From then on, for every management meeting, at whatever level, for whatever topic, the first agenda item would be Environment, Health and Safety. This sent an important signal. It also emphasised the requirement for all such meetings to have proper agendas. The signal was needed. EHS performance had been poor and there was clear evidence of supervisors allowing foolish actions and unsafe behaviour. There had been at least one fatality. The company operated in some difficult regions across the world, including the BRIC economies and parts of Eastern Europe, South America and Asia where local standards fell far short of those in the advanced economies. At board level, improved reporting put a spotlight on performance. League tables were produced and reviewed regularly. The rules of the senior management bonus plan were updated to include an EHS performance threshold, which had to be met before any bonus could even be considered. At least one regional director had his annual bonus withheld – a decision that sent powerful signals that the message had teeth and the board was serious. Throughout the organisation, the new focus meant that people did fewer foolish things. They stopped messing around in potentially dangerous production areas. Supervisors were held to account. EHS performance statistics had to be displayed on performance noticeboards at all locations. Targets were set and standards started to improve. On each chart, simple Red/Amber/Green colour coding showed current performance against target. It was a relentless journey but one that over a five-year period took group performance towards world class. There was an 80 per cent reduction in the incident and accident rate.

The tone from the top had mandated a simple change: that EHS issues were reviewed and addressed before any other operational activity was considered. By linking this to reward, the incentive mechanism sent powerful signals that changed behaviour. The group CEO would introduce the company leadership development programmes. In his introduction, he would say, 'As this is a management meeting, I'm going to start with environment, health and safety. But I'm sure you have read all the excellent slides as part of your preparatory work. If you haven't, please read them tonight. Because I'm not going to talk though the slides. Instead, I'm going to tell you what it's like to walk up to someone's front door, ring the bell and tell the lady of the house why their husband isn't coming home from work today. Or ever again'. And so he spoke, without any notes, explaining how he had met the widow of a man killed at work. In the lecture room, you could hear a pin drop. Afterwards, delegates were visibly shaken by the session and all commented on how powerfully memorable it was.

Case Study 15 – Demonstrating the Folly of Spurious Claims

Leaders who set a clear tone from the top address the need to do what's right and work to prevent what could go wrong. One company had a large customer service function. Within one department was a group of young 20-somethings. Banter was inevitable but local management made a good job of keeping it under control. One man, a person of colour, took offence at the slightest provocation. His concerns were addressed and those responsible reminded of their responsibilities. However perceptions by the complainant grew and no matter what the employer did, he found fault with it. The accusations became more racially and politically motivated until an employment tribunal claim was submitted. The employer considered the claim to be completely without foundation and did not offer to settle. The employee engaged a trade union and through them appealed to the (then) commission for racial equality. The trade union engaged a barrister so the employer had to hire a barrister as it prepared its case.

Recognising that the stakes had been raised, senior management reassured local management that they had their complete support. Having reviewed the case, all within senior management were confident. This show of support was inspirational for local managers, who feared being personally named and joined as respondents to the case.

At the tribunal, the employee's statement was inconsistent. He insisted several items of company policy had never been adhered to. Under cross-examination, he was asked why he had not raised his concerns with the employee assistance line. The employer's barrister reminded him that every employee was given a credit card-sized piece of plastic containing all the relevant contact numbers. The employee asserted that he had never been given such a card and had no knowledge of such a service. He asserted that his deliberate exclusion from the benefit was further evidence of discrimination. The barrister reminded him of the evidence previously provided. He had been briefed and every employee was given the card. At this point, and it was pure theatre, all the company observers, sitting across the full width of the room, took out their own copies of the card, gave the cards a cursory examination and returned them to their shirt or jacket pockets. The chairman of the bench saw this unrehearsed act of unison and noted it.

Under cross-examination, the employee's testimony became more and more erratic. An adjournment was called. Upon reconvening, the barrister for the employee explained that his client would not be returning to the proceedings and was withdrawing all claims. He was not seen again and did not return to work. His behaviour had been driven by emotion and, without thinking, he had taken offence to all kinds of issues. He had been foolish to pursue his case, which ultimately backfired. The tone from the top gave lasting messages: support for justice and fairness while sending a strong signal that the employer won't be held to ransom. The most enduring message was to the whole workforce: if you raise spurious claims, the company will not give in and you may not like the outcome.

Case Study 16 – Dealing with a 'Foolish Apple' who was Led on by a 'Bad Apple'

Sometimes, one has to show a willingness to fight and uphold common sense. This can be difficult where what's visible looks like a 'foolish apple' but in fact is someone being led by a 'bad apple'.

A middle-aged female worked in a department of much younger people. The culture was young, modern and direct. The lady became friendly with two young men and they enjoyed office banter together. Over a period of time, the content degenerated and eventually became rude, crude and lewd. The lady asked her friends to stop but they continued. The relationship became confused as she continued to invite them to her house on an occasional basis for a meal. Her house was substantial and a source of great pride. While she appeared friendly to them outside work, things were very different at work. She raised the issue with management who moved the two young men to a different section. However, in breaks and other social contact at work, their banter continued.

She pursued an internal complaint but this quickly led to an external employment claim. Unusually, members of management were joined as joint respondents to the claim, as well as the employer. It became apparent that the lady's claim was being driven by someone else. The force and character of the detail were not from a law firm but some other interested party. The claims became multi-dimensional, cleverly drawing in every possible aspect of employment legislation in the country concerned. It took over a year for the case to be heard. During this time, relationships had deteriorated and positions became entrenched. However, it was increasingly clear that the driving force behind the claim was the lady's husband. Under cross-examination, the two young men recounted their reaction to visiting the lady's house. It appeared much larger than anyone could reasonably expect, given the jobs she and her husband had. The two young men were very surprised. They alleged that, with some pride, the lady had explained how various extensions and structural improvements had been funded by compensation settlements extracted from her former employers. Suddenly, the motives were laid bare. The employer had offered to settle the day before the case began but the offer had been theatrically rejected. The lady was represented by her husband. As the claims started to crumble, he referred back to the offer to settle and said they would now be willing to accept it. Imagine his consternation when he was advised that, following withdrawal, the offer was simply no longer there. The case collapsed and the lady clearly felt she had been used and abused – not so much by her colleagues, but by her husband's greed and relentless pursuit of her employers. She said she realised she had been a fool and had been led astray. She should never have listened to her husband's assertions.

While the offer to settle had been a pragmatic and commercial one, it was set at about 15 per cent of the total claim. The offer had remained confidential and throughout the whole case the employer had sent very robust signals to its workforce about not tolerating improper behaviour. Training had been designed and delivered to explain the nature of harassment and how the perception of it makes it valid, irrespective of the intent. But there was another message. The employer was genuinely concerned to do the right thing, upholding the ethics of the organisation and showing that it would not give in to malicious claims. The employer had been prepared to incur very high costs, which could not be recovered from the employee in that jurisdiction. Nevertheless, it felt it was money well spent to signal justice and fairness.

Case Study 17 – Foolish Behaviour

An IT company hired a bright, young, new IT director. His technical credentials were impressive and his forceful character was clear, sharp and direct. Getting to grips with the job through the summer, he made sensible changes to structure, processes and people. He was making a good impression. Except in one area. The office premises were on an industrial estate, with no decent on-site catering. The director frequently went to a local pub at lunchtime and would return occasionally smelling of drink. Slowly but surely, members of his staff started to copy this behaviour and comments started to circulate. Within a few months, the comments had strengthened from 'I can't find employee X at lunchtime' to 'You can't get anything out of IT in the afternoons'. It was an extensive case of behaviour being copied. The director's line manager tackled the issue and warned the IT director of how perceptions had deteriorated. In return, promises were made.

In November, the local pub had a 'Beaujolais nouveau festival'. This celebrated the arrival in the UK of the first deliveries of new wine. One lunchtime, the IT director made an exception from his newfound abstinence and went to taste the newly arrived wine. Unfortunately for him, he had a minor car accident on the way back to the office. He failed the obligatory breath test and so lost his licence. As his job required multi-site working and the employer had provided the company car, his employment was ended. Almost immediately, the performance of the IT function improved, surpassing its previous best. Everyone had known of the deterioration in IT's performance under its new leader. He had a blind spot, despite being told about how he was perceived. But the signal that had been sent clearly showed the employer's stance, reinforced the rules and gave comfort to the law-abiding majority.

Reducing the Number of 'Tempted Apples'

Case Study 18 – Auditable Training Demonstrates the Tone from the Top

In 2010, the Bribery Act 2010 became law in the United Kingdom. At the time, this class-leading piece of legislation was arguably the most stringent of any jurisdiction in the world. Among many requirements, it says that UK company directors can be held to account and prosecuted for contraventions of the Act committed anywhere in the world.

A multinational operating in over 100 countries saw a clear need for education and training but there were several challenges to overcome to prevent the exercise resulting in compliance fatigue. Key questions were: How to reduce the risk of 'bad apples', 'foolish apples' and 'tempted apples'. Also, how to discharge the responsibility for training; how to deliver it in a way that people would respond enthusiastically; how to have an auditable record; how to influence the network of conversations and embed best practice in the culture. Directors also wanted to inject a sense of competition – both at a personal and divisional level – a way of getting people to think before they acted or allowed errors of omission.

A partnership between IT and HR produced a database of every email address in the company. This was then segmented by business unit. An on-line training programme was developed, translated and a communications plan was written. The training was verified by external compliance specialists. The board completed the training first. This sent a clear signal that 'What is good enough for the board should be good enough for others throughout the company'. It also sent a message that if board members can find time to complete the training, then others should be able to complete it too.

The communications programme briefed the workforce and, separately, all managers were briefed using the normal management communications channels. They were asked to set an example to their staff across the world. The email invitations were sent, giving deadlines for training completion. By clicking an embedded link, employees could choose the relevant language and then complete the training. Central monitoring showed in real time the level of uptake and completion. As a result, line managers were appraised for the completion rates in their divisions. This led to league tables of completion and that sparked some healthy rivalry.

From the outset, trainees were informed that the training would end with an on-line exam. The exam had a pass mark. On completion of the training and passing the exam, each employee was able to click an icon that said: 'Print your compliance certificate.' And they did. Local and personal healthy competition was evident as colleagues stuck their certificates to the wall or their desk panels. Junior employees showed their (higher scores than managers) certificates with pride. This infused and enthused the network of conversations across the world. For a period of three months, everyone was talking about the topic, the training and, more importantly, the issues raised. As the programme drew to a close, the league table of completion was used to hold management to account. The internal audit department was engaged to speak to managers of divisions or sections with inadequate completion rates. This prompted a final surge of completion and records showed a deep reach across and down through the entire organisation.

The benefit of this approach was that in a focused way, the tone from the top achieved culture change, compliance and a common vocabulary based on new understanding. The tone was also one of 'We are in this together and we are all doing the training programme'. It was backed up by questions during regional operational reviews so the topic was kept fresh. Special training, clear communication, injecting a sense of fun and signalling were key to the success of the programme. But it all started with the behavioural leadership of the board, which demonstrably did the training first.

A very different organisation took a similar, if somewhat more draconian approach to induction training on environment, health and safety. A series of on-line modules was developed covering several topics such risk assessments, office safety, field operations safety, energy use, environmental protection, ethics, fraud, personal safety and bomb threats. New hires received a personal welcome from the CEO explaining the requirements. An email would provide a link to the training that could be completed at any time over the new employee's first 30 days of employment. Compliance led to congratulatory messages and an alert to the line manager. Failure to complete the training successfully led to reminders regarding revision and retakes. But the most significant aspect was that if, after repeated reminders, the training was not completed, the employee's system access was locked. They were unable to access the corporate email network and system log-on was prevented. In the early days, this caused consternation. But as the word spread, growing acceptance changed the culture. Increasingly, people said 'This is what we all have to do to work here. It makes sense. If I can do it, you can do it – and you don't even need to be in the office to do it'.

This example of the tone from the top gave a strikingly simple signal about the importance of environment, health and safety. It said: 'We are serious about it. Don't get tempted to cut corners – we do things properly. We all have a common understanding that is so fundamental, it is the enabler of all the work we're required to do.'

Case Study 19 – Learning from Fraud

In the technology revolution of the early 1990s, IT systems were starting to automate business processes including pricing, discounting and payment. Personalisation was enabling companies to offer individual deals for customers large and small.

A well-known charge card company had switched to a new business service provider. As the volume of business increased, the new provider wanted to lock-in its hard-won customer with special discounts. While payment was happening electronically, the provider wanted to do something more visible in returning cash to its customer. It decided to present a cheque to its customer and create some theatre in handing it over. These were high-value cheques so processes were put in place to have the amounts verified, authorised and approved before a senior sales manager presented the refund to the customer, surrounded by a group of key people from each company. Celebratory photographs recorded the discount payment ceremony.

While the business process had focused on how to calculate the refund, raise the cheque and have it approved, not enough attention had been paid to the governance and ethics from a human perspective. No one had thought about how to mitigate the ethical risk of 'tempted apples'. No one had investigated or thought about the personal circumstances of those involved in processing the cheques. Also, no one had assessed the ethics and fraud risk of how the cheques might be intercepted and used fraudulently. Had management assessed the ethical and fraud risk more attentively, they could have prevented a very simple but effective fraud. However, the absence of such governance behaviours led to problems.

One of the individuals involved in the process had recently gone through a costly divorce. They were in financial distress and had to sell their car. Allegedly, the individual had something of an impulsive personality and was easily 'swayed' by others. The signs were there but local management had not thought through the risk of this person being a 'tempted apple'. A discount refund cheque was raised and approved for payment. All the figures were correct and it was a substantial sum. Unfortunately, the payee was printed as the name of the charge card company. This was not even followed by 'Limited, corporate account'. The employee took the cheque and paid it into their personal card account, thereby creating a massive credit balance in their name. This gave access to nearly all the money, having wiped out their balance owed to the charge card company.

The employee resigned and left rather abruptly. They then disappeared. The former employee bought three cars: one for personal use, two to sell second hand. Thankfully, police involvement brought things to a rapid conclusion. The cars had only just been registered and could successfully be 'de-registered' and returned to the dealerships. The individual was arrested, prosecuted and subsequently given a prison sentence.

The internal audit group made very strong recommendations for process, system and people changes as a result of the operational review. The learning was that one must take a much more holistic and contextual view of risk, including ethical risk. The sales and finance functions worked much more closely together after that episode. Risk assessments, tighter reference checking for new employees, special authorisations and checks were initiated. An ethics policy followed with special sections for sales and finance people.

Case Study 20 – Vision and Values Workshops

New brand identities offer great opportunities for reaffirming any organisation's commitment to ethics and setting a clear tone from the top. A new company name, for example following divestments, changes of strategy or major acquisitions, can be the launch pad for new ways of working. One newly combined organisation took this opportunity and started with a vision and values workshop at board level. The focus was on strategic goals and how they would be achieved. The board concentrated on brand values and organisational values. From there, they turned to the behaviours necessary for success in the new culture.

The very act of considering behaviour at the dawn of a new company was a rare luxury. A vision and values workshop was designed and a management training workbook produced. Starting with board members, the workshop was cascaded down through the organisation in a few weeks. The idea was that as each manager attended a session with their boss, that would act as a 'train the trainer' session for them to run the workshop with their own people. And so on down the structure. This cemented a common language and exposed the whole workforce to the same core messages in an interactive three-hour session. One of the messages addressed integrity, respect and ethics at work. Attendees were also directed to new policies that were to be published on conduct at work. While this method was not foolproof, it did put down a marker for change and provided clear guidance to all on what was expected at work. Above all, the workshop explained that values exist to guide behaviour in situations where there are no rules.

In the research for Part I of this book, one chairman said that all the company's work on ethics and the tone from the top would be worthwhile if at a point of pressure a front-line employee stops and thinks about a request to 'stuff the channel', that is, by shipping next month's order this month. He felt that if more employees would stop and ask 'What is the right thing to do?' then the work on ethics would be well spent. This case study shows a concern to do just that. Ethics were reinforced through an emphasis on values and behaviour.

What Gets in the Way

Case Study 21 – Taking Too Long to Complete Post-merger Integration

Sometimes organisations can lose sight of higher objectives. In the pursuit of a particular tone from the top – for example fairness, consistency and due consideration – other parameters may be overlooked – such as speed of execution. One example was the five-way merger that merged Mercury, Bell Cable Media, NyNex, Videotron and Anite. The UK telecommunications industry had grown rapidly following deregulation. Some commentators referred to an explosion of providers. The cable TV companies which had a large local loop connection to homes started offering phone services as well as TV. As with many industries, after deregulation, the explosion is followed by an implosion – or consolidation. The aim was to act as the consolidator of the sector in the UK, with business communications providing the cash flow and consumer telecoms providing the growth.

The five companies were therefore to be merged into one listed company, which at its peak employed 18,000 people and was in the FTSE 50. From a purely statistical point of view, as a manager, one had a one-in-five chance of keeping one's job. So it was a high-stakes, high-stress environment. The organisation design was planned in phases, from the top down. After all, it makes sense for newly appointed leaders to have a say in who is on their team. However, in pursuit of high ethical standards of selection without discrimination, the company lost its way. Organisation design was subject to executive oversight. The top team was still bedding down and vested interests had not been ironed out. Insufficient attention was paid to taking cost out and in some cases instructions on increasing spans of control were, perhaps wilfully, misinterpreted as putting more jobs into the structure rather than stripping out management positions. The notion of a span of control of 15 – that is, a manager should be able to manage a team of 15 – was seen in some areas as 'I can now hire people to fill more slots!'

All management positions were subject to external executive assessment. This was a massive contract for a tier one head-hunter. It was a thorough process but it took time. Candidates were subject to psychometric testing, 360-degree feedback and a three-hour competency-based interview. Reports were submitted, compared and considered. With each successive wave of appointments, a new level was completed in the structure. The fall-out from that was a large number of surplus people looking for redeployment in other areas or even at the next level down. This created a burden and a distraction, although those displaced rightly merited professional treatment. An outplacement process went into full gear. Redeployees were fed into the remaining selection processes. Those who were successful were legally entitled to a trial period without loss of redundancy rights. And some people 'gamed' the system to prolong their tenure in the hope of finding a more suitable role.

By the time the reorganisation was complete, more than six months had passed and a somewhat-less-than healthy internal focus caused the new company to take its eye off the ball. The unintended consequence was a tone from the top that was seen as too slow, insufficiently entrepreneurial and process-heavy. Within three years, the business was being separated into a business-to-business company and a consumer company. The consumer company would ultimately be sold to NTL, which in turn became Virgin Media.

Case Study 22 – Politics and Personal Agendas

In another organisation, a new divisional head was appointed to shake things up. The company in question was experiencing fundamental market change as competition intensified, prices fell and on-line self-service devoured margins. One commentator said: 'The last thing this company needs is a strategy, we just need to take cost out as fast as we can.' Another said: 'When the plane is in a nose dive, the last thing we want to do is try and serve a hot meal.'

Business process outsourcing was in vogue and new service providers were clamouring to get a slice of the action. The new head seized the opportunity and saw a fast route to major cost reduction and also the variablization of cost. The tone from the top was one of speed, bold moves and challenging all sacred cows. But insufficient attention was paid to reputation management and the ethics of the decision started to be questioned. People felt it was being implemented too fast. They alleged lip service was being paid to legitimate concerns. There was open speculation about the wives of the CEO and the outsource head having lunch together. Proposals for setting up an in-house version of what was offered by the outsourcer were given short shrift.

The decision was felt to be a *fait accompli* and a sense of being 'railroaded' prevailed. Certainly, radical action was required but, as is so often the case, it is not so much the 'what' but the 'how' that determine the ethics perceived by the court of public opinion. Some employees felt that the new executive was overly keen to make his mark through bold strategic moves, come what may. Numerous employees transferred to the outsource provider. They were told that they 'were still part of the same team, just part of a different economic entity'. However they felt they had been moved to a very different culture. The different management regime had a much more mechanistic style. As process automation proceeded, the knowledge and experience of the transferred people was built into the system. As labour turnover took its course, replacement people came in at half the cost of their predecessors. While this made sound economic sense, the customers of the service felt it had degraded to little more than a call centre.

Meanwhile, the client company felt the outsource provider needed tight management from a contractual perspective. The client had estimated it would need one person to manage the contractual relationship, verify billing and approve payments. This was an underestimate and over a period of time the contract management team grew to six people. It was alleged that large volumes of unplanned invoicing was taking place, all of which needed checking. Perhaps the client had not fully appreciated the provider's need for rigorous standardisation, as well as their need to make a profit. For example, standard reports were produced for local managers. Some asked for the content to be presented in a different, more familiar format. The outsourcer obliged but at a cost of several hundred pounds per report.

The tone from the top was one of speed and cost reduction come what may. At the sharp end, it was alleged that certain issues were brushed aside, in the interests of achieving major change. The way in which decisions were made was seen as less than perfect. At the end of the contracted period, the service was brought back in-house. From a behavioural perspective, one was left wondering whether a different, more inclusive tone might have led to a better outcome.

Case Study 23 – Capital Projects and the Tone from the Top

Many companies implement ambitious IT web enablement projects. These aim to automate back office functionality, providing employee self-service and customer self-service. Long gone are the days when a travel agent would send through the post a four-part air ticket, complete with layers of carbon paper. A senior executive was project sponsor for an IT enablement project. This would automate multiple business processes and take out labour cost. However, rather than see it as a people-change management project, the sponsor viewed it as a technology project. As a result, it was assumed that the IT technologists would look after the key issues. Unfortunately, line managers highlighted all kinds of reasons why their way of running the business process should become the one new way. Competing arguments surfaced but were not resolved. The sponsor did not establish his credentials and did not give a clear tone from the top. In fact operational issues tended to push project sponsorship to the bottom of the agenda. Line management perceived the project as an unnecessary intrusion. The sponsor could have set a clear tone from the top by demonstrating leadership and a firm operational grip, allaying managements' fears, acting in anticipation of what any external scrutiny might find and understanding how the project might fail – either in part or in full.

The clear opportunity was to gain regular first-hand information on progress, to review the effectiveness of communications, to see exactly how the organisation was working and develop an early warning system. This in turn could have helped to identify issues and remedial action, training requirements and areas needing more support. All these things could have enhanced the sponsor's effectiveness and reputation. Unfortunately, the business impact was not understood and process knock-on problems came to the surface. While the project's business case and definition report were good, the governance processes were not effective. This, perhaps above all other factors, prevented a clear leadership tone; there was no drumbeat of action, progress and review.

The project went over budget and into remedial action to recover lost ground, lost functionality, lost time and lost confidence. All of this could have been avoided. Instead of the leader taking the opportunity to enhance his executive presence, it was lost. The lasting impression was of someone not quite up to the challenge. A CEO once said to me that every effective executive has a 'Plan B, a Plan C, the outline of a Plan D and a sketch of Plan E'. She or he recognises that nothing ever goes to plan and so they move with apparent ease to the next plan, to keep results coming in on time. Another chief executive said he thought there should only be two things that should get people fired:

one was poor ethics such as through low-integrity behaviour (including dishonesty, fraud, theft); the other was failing to ask for help.

Case Study 24 – Problem-solving by Separating Perception from Fact

A large service company employing thousands of people had been taken private. Away from the spotlight of a public listing, costs were stripped out and efficiency improved. The company went on the acquisition trail and acquired many smaller competitors. Later it relisted as a public limited company but had a lack of infrastructure. As the acquisitions were integrated, both functions and people were brought closer together, sometimes being co-located for the first time. The employee survey raised increasing concerns about fairness of reward. Local discrepancies were discussed but there was no central action. The CEO decided to address the problem, showing and communicating a clear tone from the top. It was one of pragmatism, set against a background of economic difficulty and little if any 'new money' to buy the company out of any problems.

Up to now, management had not known what to do or how to investigate the alleged problems. External help was brought in. This showed independence and impartiality from the chief executive, who was keen to demonstrate there would be no pre-determined outcome. An externally facilitated workshop involving cross-functional stakeholders drew up an action plan to gather data, analyse it and propose solutions. Management were informed of what was being investigated and why it was important for them to cooperate and provide information on request. The data collection revealed some clear outliers in the pay distribution. However, it also revealed different mixes of fixed and variable pay. These differences were fuelling perceptions of the differences being much wider differences that was actually the case. The action plans harmonised terms and conditions, simplified the variable reward mechanisms and put the company on a firm footing for more consistent reward. A small number of outliers were addressed individually and a simple grading structure was put in. Communications then followed, to equip managers with knowledge and information on how to explain the perceptions, why people had drawn certain conclusions and how the company was addressing the matter without breaking the bank.

By using external, independent help, setting a clear tone about supporting fairness, setting realistic economic boundaries and then stepping back, the chief executive recognised the need for action, trusting management to produce recommendations for solutions. In accepting them, he showed support and helped to drive the solution.

ON LEADERSHIP

Part I of this book presented the research into *The Tone from the Top*. Part II gave examples from around the world of the varying degrees to which some organisations have upheld their ethical compass. Part III now addresses issues of leadership and how leaders can display personal commitment to ethical business without diluting the pursuit of success. It also offers advice on how to avoid leadership traps and mistakes – some of which arise from ethical dilemmas. The enduring theme is that behaviour is a core hallmark of leadership. In today's world, organisations increasingly call for characteristics such as:

- Curiosity
- Insight
- Engagement
- Determination

These characteristics must be visible to a great extent in the behaviour of the leader. Curiosity is the desire to seek out new knowledge, experience and candid feedback on how leaders are perceived. Being open to change and to learning shows flexibility and encourages it in others. Insight is the ability to gather and make sense of information that can suggest new approaches, new possibilities and new solutions. Engagement is about how leaders use emotion as well as logic to inspire others, connect with a wide audience and communicate a persuasive vision of the future. Determination is about how leaders strive for challenging goals and the extent to which they can bounce back from adversity or setbacks.

Classical theories of management tended to focus on control versus empowerment but few paid attention to how leadership should mitigate ethical risk. McGregor's 'Theory X and Theory Y' explained how in Theory X, an authoritarian, directive and at times repressive style, was based on tight control. It assumed that the average person prefers to be directed, avoids responsibility, is relatively unambitious and wants security and predictability. 'Theory X' environments often have a culture of telling people what to do with the unintended consequence of people always needing to be told what to do. A repressive culture then has people find ways around rules and tight control – almost encouraging them to look for ethical loopholes to exploit. In 'Theory Y' the culture is based on participative management. The assumption is that people will apply self-control and self-direction in the pursuit of organisational objectives. There is little need for external control or the threat of punishment. It assumes people usually accept and often seek responsibility. 'Theory Y' is therefore seen as more enabling through empowerment. It is liberating and developmental with control being achieved through giving responsibility. But it does not necessarily mitigate ethical risk because foolish apples and tempted apples frequently don't know what they don't know.

John Adair's Action Centred Leadership provides a simple model in which three elements combine in intersecting circles: Task, Team and Individual needs. Action-centred leadership does address ethics, suggesting that delegation is proportional to trust, based on sound understanding of maturity and capability.

Task: the key responsibilities of the leader for achieving the task are listed as identifying the aims, vision, purpose and direction to define the task. Then the leader must identify resources, people, processes, systems, tools and create a plan to achieve the task. Next is establishing responsibilities, objectives, accountabilities and measures. Thereafter, the responsibilities include setting standards, quality, time and reporting parameters, monitoring and control to maintain performance against plan. Finally come review, reassessment, adjusting the plan and targets as necessary.

Team: the key responsibilities of the leader for achieving team needs are given as: to establish, agree and communicate standards of performance and behaviour and to establish the style, culture and approach of the team. Next is to monitor and maintain discipline, ethics and integrity and to anticipate then resolve team conflict or disagreement. The leader should assess and change the balance of the team as necessary and develop the collective maturity and capability of the team. The leader progressively increases team freedom and authority, motivates the team and provides a collective sense of purpose. The leader identifies, develops and agrees team and project leadership roles and meets identified developmental needs. The leader gives the team feedback on overall progress.

Individual: here, the leader understands each team member and assists with supporting them individually, on plans, problems and challenges. The leader identifies and agrees appropriate individual responsibilities and objectives, giving recognition or praise where merited. The leader rewards individuals with extra responsibilities and objectives and develops them. The leader identifies each individual's capabilities and strengths, and trains and develops them to provide greater freedom and authority. In this way the leader can monitor the ethical compass of each individual.

ON LEADERSHIP

THE EVOLUTION OF THE LEADER'S ROLE THROUGH ONE'S CAREER

The diagram in Figure 1 has two axes: the horizontal axis shows a mix of skills required for success. The vertical axis shows increasing seniority from low to high. Early in our careers, our success is determined largely by the quality and quantity of 'task' that we execute. Certainly, interpersonal skills are required and emotional intelligence highly beneficial, but most of our actual work is based on task delivery. As we get more senior, the balance starts to shift. Our ability to build, sustain and influence relationships becomes more important. As we manage more people and reach leadership positions, the role of 'task' is in the minority; most of our success is predicated on the quality of relationships. And yet I have met many very senior executives, including some at board level, who have not quite understood the importance of the 'shadow' they cast, how to use that to influence others and extend their ethical reputation via their tone from the top. Some have said to me that they are 'employees just like anyone else'. Others said they expected compliance because the governance processes mandated it, so little was required from personal example. Others, again, had difficulty seeing how subordinate managers were profoundly influenced by the slightest nuance of speech, by body language and by what was not said. For example, a fleeting corridor comment from a main board member was remembered for years afterwards. The tone from the top lived and breathed in the persona of the leader but they had not appreciated it. Similarly, I have met others who appear to operate at a much lower level in the diagram than their position rightly demands. A strong work ethic and a prodigious work output had brought success and promotion. Good, rational decisions had delivered promotion. But once in a senior leadership position, some people hang onto what I call retained hobbies, get into unnecessary detail and fail to delegate enough. I once came across a group CFO who felt the need to check the entire head office payroll.

Some leaders fail to operate at the right level, instead preferring to focus on task more than relationships

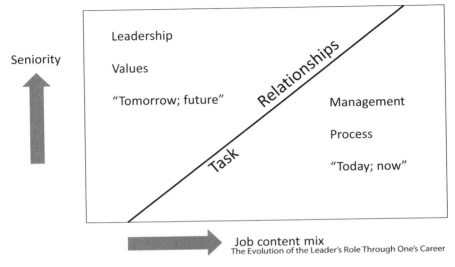

Job content mix
The Evolution of the Leader's Role Through One's Career

Figure 1   **Leadership evolution through one's career**

As leaders move up the diagram, most learn that influence and effectiveness are increasingly predicated on who you are rather than the office one holds. In the end, hectoring or unspoken threats won't inspire discretionary extra effort. People tend to follow leaders because of their authenticity, their ethics and the tone from the top that these things communicate. Leadership is about behaviour, relying on less tangible or measurable things like values, trust, inspiration, attitude, the way decisions are made and personal character. In particular, where a leader has a strong value-set and consistently lives those values, employees are more likely to ask themselves in times of ambiguity, 'What would the leader do?' Where such employees are presented with an ethical dilemma, they are more likely to rely on the values of the leader and either follow those, or ask the question: 'How would (the leader) approach this and what risks are apparent?' Values are particularly powerful in situations where there are no formal rules. Where rules cannot be created for every situation, values give powerful guidance in the form of the tone from the top. An additional benefit is that the stronger the values are lived, the smaller the need for large rulebooks. People intuitively know what are the things and behaviours that get people promoted versus fired. For example, at Netflix, the entire expenses policy says 'Act in Netflix's best interests'.

Management on the other hand is more about process. It relies heavily on tangible, measurable capabilities such as planning, organising, use of organisational systems, monitoring, validating and using appropriate communication methods.

A research organisation wanted to understand more about what employees want from their leaders at work. The questions asked are what are the attributes that people most value from their leaders? There have been many studies of leadership but few on followers and their expectations of leadership. I believe this is where a strong tone from the top follows directly from leadership responding to their followers' expectations and requirements. The researchers undertook thousands of workplace interviews. These produced tens if not hundreds of thousands of answers. However in distilling them down, it quickly became apparent that there were just a few categories of requirement. These were subsequently narrowed to just four things:

1. Tell me the truth
2. Keep me safe
3. Show me you care
4. Give me hope.

1: Tell me the truth. This is an appeal not just for honesty and clarity, but also to be treated as adults. Interestingly it is also an appeal for adult behaviour on the part of the leader. How many times have we seen strong leaders go to pieces when having to announce to a town hall meeting or an all-employee audio that redundancies or layoffs are going to happen? People are more likely to believe difficult messages if they are confident in the leader delivering the message. So quality of delivery and the message received are as important as the content. The bigger the audience, the simpler the message needs to be.

2: Keep me safe. This is a request for safety at several different levels. At its simplest, it is an appeal for a safe working environment without incident, accident or injury. But there is more to it, and here's why: it is an appeal from followers for their leaders to act in their interests. Lord Dannatt, formerly General Sir Richard Dannatt, once said that all leaders have the ability to take their followers to places they did not expect to go to and might not even want to go to. He said leaders have a vision which they can articulate. They get us to buy into that vision. They can do this because the followers give them legitimacy. And that in turn comes from the followers' conviction that the leader represents their best interests. Simply barking out orders does not work in a Wiki World of instant, free and empowering information available to almost anyone. It therefore follows that leaders will be followed for as long as the followers believe the leader is acting in their best interests. Without that, it becomes increasingly difficult for any leader to rely on discretionary extra effort from their people. Safety is therefore physical, contextual, emotional, political and organisational.

3: Show me you care. This request is for leadership to show personal interest in individuals and their contribution to the organisation. In a discussion about performance management many years ago, a middle manager said to me: 'When the formal appraisal process stops – perhaps due to managerial failings or the employer no longer supporting it, you give a big sigh of relief. The second time there is no performance review, you get frustrated because you don't know how you are doing. The third time it doesn't happen is the last because you are actively looking to leave.' Taking an interest in the individual sends a message about the follower's relationship with the leader and the employer. From the Hawthorne experiment in the 1920s to today's managers as coaches, people respond better when someone takes an interest in them.

4: Give me hope. This does not mean followers are suffering from depression. Far from it, they want to be inspired. They want a tone from the top that sets aspirational standards, mitigates risk and addresses the inevitable setbacks. Followers were asking for a reason to believe in the future success of the organisation. All too often, the history of organisations is written by the disasters that befall them. I think it was Churchill who said 'success is going from failure to failure without loss of enthusiasm'. Recognising that people are there to solve problems and make things better, it is perhaps the role of leadership to inspire people to want to address thorny issues and overcome difficulty. The tone from the top can give hope by signalling a strong work ethic, justice and fairness, the absence of discrimination and harnessing of diversity, to name a few. The tone can also signal that leadership won't put up with dishonesty, improper conduct, incapability, fraud or not doing the right thing. A strong tone from the top gives hope that issues will be resolved and leadership is acting in the best interests of followers.

Some leaders fail to realise how senior they have become. They don't 'get it' in terms of their responsibilities for behaviour, ethics and role modelling. They don't appreciate the impact their whole person has on others and organisational performance. And yet they are always on duty, always under scrutiny and always open to judgement – typically from an ever-widening group of individuals. This is why safeguarding one's reputation as a leader is so important. One of the best ways of doing that is to have a strong value-set, display strong ethics and have a clear personal tone from the top. Perhaps some of the most effective advice to aspiring leaders is to help them model the transition to a leadership state of mind and behaviour. Many fail to see this transition and land a leadership role still thinking they can behave as 'one of the gang'. If executive presence is the ability to multiply one's contribution by one's impact on others, all leaders should develop understanding and self-awareness of how their executive presence is viewed and experienced. I met one leader who used the diagram in Figure 1 to conduct a 360-degree feedback exercise. He asked colleagues at various levels, including his boss, to show on the diagram the level at which he was operating and also the level which his job required. He then noted differences in perception both in the answers from each person and between people. This helped him to model the role of a leader more effectively and focus on a more appropriate tone from the top.

'THE THREE C MODEL' FOR LEADERSHIP SETTING THE TONE FROM THE TOP

I have worked with executive head-hunters over many years, recruiting roles up to CEO and non-executive positions. I always asked for the head-hunter's view of the core characteristics they looked for in great candidates. As you can imagine, there was a long list. All aspects were valid and relevant in the circumstances. Distilling the collected wisdom to really basic things, I concluded on a 'three C model' which is illustrated in Figure 2:

- Confidence
- Competence
- Commitment

Linkage between competencies searched for by headhunters and Lean tools

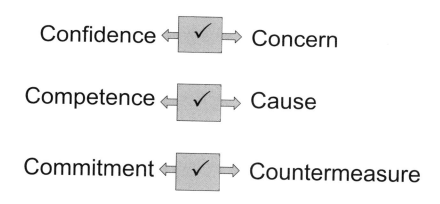

Great executives display confidence, competence and commitment. Lean tools analyse concerns: what is deficient, defective or sub-optimal. Root cause analysis gets to the real issue. Countermeasures put in sustainable solutions that endure. Even at board level, it takes confidence to raise concerns, it takes competence to get to the real root cause and it takes commitment to ensure countermeasures work long term.

Figure 2   'The three C model' for leadership setting the tone from the top

Confidence in this model includes such topics as executive presence, influence, drive, volunteering ideas and managing the agenda. It's also about seizing the moment and driving action. Further, it is about the kind of confidence that comes from having done one's homework. When you are sure of your facts, that gives a certain confidence. It is not about over-confidence, hubris or false confidence, having failed to assess situations correctly. It is certainly not about arrogance.

Competence covers the topics of knowing one's brief, being fully up-to-date and seeking out knowledge and information. This covers the need for breadth and the ability to see the connections that others can't. It also includes experience and the learning that comes from experience. Competence is not just subject-specific competence. It very much is about interpersonal competence, emotional intelligence and the ability to influence with integrity.

Commitment in this model is all about ethical commitment, commitment to doing the right thing. Once the intellectual and ethical aspects are clear, there is also the issue of stamina – both intellectual and physical, to stay with a task or project to completion. To an extent, it includes energy and the impact one has on others. People have often said to me that they are inspired by others who make them feel as if they have just plugged into the mains to recharge their own batteries. Commitment is also about not shirking the difficult decisions. This reflects the value-set of the individual and the more visible that is, the more likely the tone from the top will have traction.

No doubt you could choose other words for your own model but I am sure there will be areas of overlap. And there is more. In Lean systems, Lean manufacturing and Lean process work there is another 'three C model'. Having worked with this for several years, I had a personal 'Ah-ha' moment when I saw the linkage to my first 'three C model'. The Lean 'three C model' is:

- Concern
- Cause
- Countermeasure

Concern is about what is actually happening, defining a problem or a defective process. In other words, 'What is the problem?' It is also about raising the concern so it can be addressed. There are processes and tools to refine the concern and make sure one really has defined what it is and is not.

Cause, as the word suggests, is about the root cause analysis of the problem. This includes doing sufficient analysis to be sure one has the full cause, the root cause, rather than symptoms or what may appear to be the cause of the problem.

Countermeasure is about corrective action to resolve the issue, fix the cause and remove the concern. Countermeasures may be a one-off, a series of steps or a process intervention. Countermeasures may be physical or virtual, hard and soft. They could be component based or human skill based.

The linkage between these two models was instructive. First, it takes confidence to raise an issue, or alert others to a concern. This may sound simple but I have watched board members in several countries who were reluctant to speak up about legitimate concerns. As one of the case studies showed, a business plan was described as a 'walk in the park', when that was far from reality. I have known other directors who did not have the confidence to raise a concern with their CEO, with the non-executive directors or the chair. An effective tone from the top should set an environment in which meetings at all levels, especially board meetings, are safe places to raise concerns.

Secondly, it takes real competence to get to the cause of what's going wrong. Many times, I have come across executives who go straight to a solution. In their time-pressed world where success is (wrongly) measured by how many things they can clear from their in-box each day, such people can jump to the wrong conclusion. The ability to step back, reflect and apply one's experience to issues can set a tone that says 'Do it once, do it properly, do it right'. And that does not mean taking forever. Even a carpenter will measure twice to cut once.

Thirdly, it takes commitment to deliver countermeasures that last. This is especially true for countermeasures requiring human intervention. Whether it is checking that instructions have been understood and carried out, verifying the learning from training or performing due diligence on a culture change programme, follow through is required. In a busy world, it is all too easy to rely on expectation and assumption that one's view of the countermeasures required has been fully understood and acted upon.

With both 'three C models' working and interacting together, I believe they help leaders set a strong tone from the top. It is a tone that says the organisation is professional, keeps its promises, does the right thing, upholds ethical practice and has the strength to deliver. Perhaps of greater importance, these models help leaders set a tone that mitigates ethical risk by encouraging people at all levels to raise concerns – whether physical or ethical. The focus is on resolution, via analysis of root cause. But it also addresses correction to prevent the concern happening again. This mix of process and behavioural traits can be a powerful tool for mitigating ethical risk.

LEADERSHIP PITFALLS

In setting a tone from the top, founded on values and the 'three C models' above, there remains the risk of poor leaders undermining the tone. I have observed several CEOs who had to remove people who displayed poor behaviour or who were simply not aligned to the ethical tone being implemented. I'm not advocating intolerance of diversity or the denial of dissent; 'groupthink' can be as dangerous as dysfunctionality from warring factions. But most bad leaders display poor behaviour. The challenge is when to deal with it. Sadly, and all too often, senior leaders are reluctant to deal with bad behaviour, especially where financial performance remains strong. At a major big four consulting firm, a senior partner had been bringing in £15m of business a year. Colleagues however thought he was untouchable because he brought in so much business. If he left, he would no doubt take those clients with him to the competition. But his behaviour was no longer tolerable. The managing partner spoke to him, explaining the situation. Contrary to expectation, the partner said no one had ever spoken to him before to give such guidance. He realised that he could be fired and a behavioural change programme was put in place. Because it was handled well, the individual improved both his behaviour and his commercial performance, delivering record revenue the following year.

The best leaders are most aware of what they are not good at. Through self-awareness they compensate for their weaker areas and blind spots by surrounding themselves with complementary skills. In this way, they use team skills and effectiveness to counterbalance what they are not good at. The best leaders display humility as well as an intense will. This can set a tone from the top that focuses on performance in a context of one only being as good as the people who work for you.

A CEO promoted the notion of financial performance no longer being good enough. He said, 'from now on, you have to get more than one tick in one box'. There were to be three boxes: great financial performance, great people management and great customer experience. This came as something of a culture shock for some country managers, who previously thought the ends would justify the means – their focus had been on delivering revenue, profit, margin, operating cash flow and cost reduction. Their newly expanded remit was a challenge but it led to a more sustainable business.

What are the most common development needs of leaders? It could be argued that they are in managing relationships – a topic covered in Figure 1 earlier. To be more specific, several commentators list the following, illustrated in Figure 3:

- Empathy
- Developing others
- Conflict management

Empathy is not simply showing you care. It is about learning how to listen and show you are listening even when you don't have time. It is about demonstrating awareness of how others are feeling, not just awareness of what they are saying. This provides context and understanding. It is about building and sustaining rapport even when under time pressure from many other demands.

Most bad leaders have poor behaviour

- The best leaders are most aware of what they are <u>not</u> good at

- The best display humility as well as intense will

The three most common development needs of leaders:

Hierarchy of leadership capability

- Empathy – Demonstrating an awareness of how people are feeling

- Developing others – identifying opportunities and stimulating people to develop to their full potential

- Conflict management – Spotting potential conflict, bringing disagreements into the open and helping to de-escalate them

Figure 3   Leadership pitfalls

Developing others refers to identifying opportunities and stimulating people to develop to their full potential. Such opportunities could be small, short term or large and career defining over the long term. Great leaders are constantly on the look-out for opportunities for their people to grow. They give constant encouragement to inspire them. Again, this refers to one being only as good as the people who work for you. It sets a tone from the top of development, learning and progress. These concepts speak to some fundamental issues about what drives people at work. Handled successfully, these can build much more sustainable workplaces, where people at all levels feel a sense of autonomy, mastery and purpose.

Conflict management refers to the ability to spot potential conflict ahead of it happening, then bringing issues out into the open. Having done that, great leaders help to de-escalate the issues, removing heat and emotion while helping others build a constructive way forward. This quality refers to conflict management at all levels. It is perhaps most important in leadership teams and boards. It is a particular skill for chairmen. I believe this ability is one of the most important behavioural aspects in setting the tone from the top.

In the hierarchy of leadership capability, one could say that the entry level includes matters of intellect. This is based on rationality, that is, what's logical and sensible. The next level up is based on emotion – recognising one's own and those of others, then responding to emotion in ways that engage people. Such engagement is more powerful than being based on logic alone. It is behavioural. Signals sent by behaviour contribute significantly to an effective tone from the top. Finally, at the top of our hierarchy of leadership capability are transpersonal issues. These go beyond ego. This is where great leaders show humility as well as intense will. They are not leading for their own self-promotion, but for the greater good of the organisation and wider society. Such characteristics are frequently based on values and ethics. Again, this should be a large element of the tone from the top. Leaders with transpersonal behaviour often set a tone of selflessness in the pursuit of organisational goals. They also promote the notion of 'the organisation first'.

BEYOND RATIONALITY

Figure 4 shows another model I have used to help leaders. I call it my RIEPP model. This invites leaders to consider issues or problems from multiple perspectives. It starts with what's rational. Objectivity and getting the facts are paramount here. The second part is to consider the issue from the perspective of the irrational. The value of this is to force leaders to think about things from the opposite point of view and gain additional insights. For example, if you are leading a pharmaceutical business and are facing disruption from animal rights protesters, it might be helpful to get inside their minds to understand how best to deal with the disruption. The third part is to consider issues from a purely emotional perspective. By understanding underlying emotions, one can gain better insights.

Leaders should consider the psychological landscape that governs behaviour

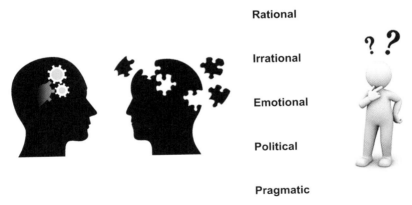

Rational

Irrational

Emotional

Political

Pragmatic

Figure 4   Beyond rationality

For example, I once faced an irate senior executive whose anger and frustration were wholly disproportionate to the matter being raised. Whichever aspect we tried to discuss, the reaction was excessive for no apparent reason. A main board director had said to me, 'context is everything'. Remembering this, I sought to understand what the emotional context was. It turned out that the executive was going through a traumatic and financially horrendous divorce. It was consuming her very being.

The fourth part is to review the issue from a political perspective. This refers to team politics, organisational politics, stakeholder politics and, if necessary, the wider political, governmental or regulatory political landscape. I sit in a non-executive role on the remuneration and appointments committee of a regulator. We were debating when and how we should review the fees for the non-executive directors. The discussion reviewed policy, market forces, what other regulators do and which ones had reviews pending. After a significant amount of time spent discussing the rational, logical and numerical issues, it was my turn to speak. I said that we should first review the policy to update the committee on the circumstances and methodology for conducting a review. Then, we should be clear on what market data we would rely on to inform any decision when it becomes due. However, the single most important factor was that in the court of public opinion, no increase would find favour in the current climate. It was therefore for this reason, and despite all the logic, that it was not appropriate to proceed with any review, however justified it might appear from the data. Some members of the committee felt uncomfortable with this. They considered the power of the rational argument to be sufficient. However the chair intervened, confirming that it would not be politically acceptable to implement a review now or within the next 12 months.

The final part is to take stock of the previous considerations: rational, irrational, emotional and political. Then, by means of a synthesis guided by ethics, to consider what in all the circumstances would be the pragmatic and right solution. The value of this is to implement a pragmatic solution, based on full consideration of a much wider contextual landscape than otherwise would have been the case. Pragmatism does not necessarily mean a compromise. It means doing the right thing in a way that has the greatest chance of success. Or as one former general once said: 'an imperfect plan, ruthlessly executed has a far greater chance of success than a perfect plan executed in an imperfect way.' Perfection may take a little longer but appropriate steps and a sense of progress are important, especially in maintaining the tone from the top.

DYSFUNCTIONAL LEADERSHIP

The Financial Reporting Council gives guidance on how directors should perform their roles and how boards should be evaluated. The following are offered for inclusion in evaluations of board effectiveness:

- The mix of skills, experience, knowledge and diversity on the board, in the context of the challenges facing the company
- Clarity of, and leadership given to, the purpose, direction and values of the company
- Succession and development plans; how the board works together as a unit, and the tone set by the chairman and the CEO
- Key board relationships, particularly chairman/CEO, chairman/senior independent director, chairman/company secretary and executive/non-executive
- Effectiveness of individual non-executive and executive directors
- Clarity of the senior independent director's role
- Effectiveness of board committees, and how they are connected with the main board
- Quality of the general information provided on the company and its performance
- Quality of papers and presentations to the board
- Quality of discussions around individual proposals
- Process the chairman uses to ensure sufficient debate for major decisions or contentious issues
- Effectiveness of the secretariat
- Clarity of the decision processes and authorities
- Processes for identifying and reviewing risks and
- How the board communicates with, and listens to, shareholders and other stakeholders

In my consulting business, I am sometimes asked about the warning signs of top team dysfunctionality. Typically, I focus on behaviour more than process, although both are important. In reviewing what seems to be going wrong, it can be helpful to ask the following questions:

a) Are there problems in reaching decisions? Understanding why decisions are not getting made helps get the so-called elephant onto the table. At least there is then a chance that it can be addressed.
b) Is there any evidence of friction or an 'us and them' culture? This might be between executive and non-executive directors or between a CEO and Chair or between directors in rival camps, emanating perhaps from a merger or takeover.
c) Is there insufficient factual information in order to make decisions? Sometimes people rely on alleged experience, gut feel or their certain knowledge that a project is the right thing to do but others are not persuaded.
d) Is the nature of board discussion backward looking? If too much time is

spent on historic reporting, the 'rear view mirror' syndrome tends to crowd-out consideration of strategic future opportunities.

e) Are contributors rehearsing old arguments? This happens where the un-persuaded dwell on previous points and revisit arguments, refusing to move on.

f) Is there 'campaigning?' This aspect is subtly different and best described as people getting on their hobbyhorse to campaign repeatedly for a known point of view or course of action.

g) Is there a dismissive 'flavour of the month' attitude to ideas? Sometimes an excessive focus on what could go wrong, what won't work or can't work here can stifle innovation.

h) Is the answer not remotely related to the question? This is where there is a dialogue of the deaf and it can be quite comical. Unrelated monologues can play table tennis against each other when no one steps in to stop it. If ever you have observed people in terms of 'There are those who listen and those who simply wait to speak', you will understand this point very well.

i) Is the environment the wrong sort? In particular, is there an absence of both challenge *and* support? One without the other is dysfunctional as we will see in the next diagram. The absence of both is insidiously toxic.

j) Is inaccurate, incomplete or out-of-date information being presented? Some markets move much faster than traditional reporting cycles. So it's important to match the rhythm and pace of the business with information that informs future action not the history books.

k) When was the last new service or product launched? If the organisation has not delivered innovation to its chosen markets in years, it is moving backwards rapidly. This is particularly true if competitors are actively and visibly innovative.

l) Is there a sense that staff 'don't understand or communicate our vision effectively?' If so, there may be serious communication and engagement failings … from the top.

m) Do directors feel unprepared and often surprised? Where this happens, they are probably not on top of their game. There may be a mismatch between the rhythm and pace of the business and the way governance and reporting, business reviews and information are provided to the senior team.

n) Finally, if any member of a senior team considers that board meetings are boring, covering the 'same old, same old', there may be serious blind spots in which process and governance have overshadowed agenda space for more open discussion, free thinking and debate on strategic matters. Or as one executive said: 'If a director can't take their eye off their iPhone for more than five minutes, how can I trust her or him to keep an eye on future strategy?'

If your senior team, executive committee or board display two or more of the characteristics shown in Figure 5, action needs to be taken. These characteristics include not enough structure, a lack of strategic focus, being backward-looking and not spending enough time on value creation. Further, teams can suffer from 'group think' in which the absence of diverse views causes everyone to persuade themselves of the validity of their one true way. It is alleged that executives at Blackberry were considering the competitive threat from Apple before it launched the very first iPhone. A technical report had said it was not possible to store enough battery power to light a touch screen display of the intended size for more than half a day. The threat was therefore not really credible. After the iPhone was launched, apparently, at a board meeting, Blackberry directors were examining the product, having bought them in the open market. One executive accidentally dropped his on the floor. The glass screen was seriously cracked. He picked it up, allegedly saying, 'I don't think we have to worry about the iPhone'.

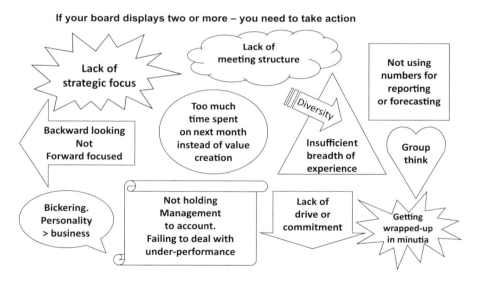

Figure 5   Dysfunctional leadership and pitfalls for boards to avoid

This example is for me one of the best reasons why top team diversity is so important. I am not simply talking about gender diversity but diversity in all its richness: culture, race, ethnicity, gender, perspective, context, experience and sectors. Certainly, having more women on boards is bringing fresh perspectives. One commentator even went as far as saying just one woman on a board yielded a 20 per cent lower chance of the company going bankrupt. But in this iPhone example, there was collective denial of the game-changer before their very eyes.

Boards that fail to hold management to account or which fail to deal with under-performance send signals down the organisation which devalue the tone from the top, replacing it with one of mediocrity. That is dangerous because it can also imply that ethical mediocrity will be tolerated. Skirting over non-conformity, poor compliance or poor performance can therefore lead to more difficulty. One senior executive once said to me: 'The time to deal with a problem is before it becomes a bigger problem.'

Research on board evaluation ('Board Evaluation' published jointly by my consulting firm Keeldeep Associates Limited and Ashridge Business School) interviewed the chairmen of 30 FTSE200 companies. Chairmen broadly felt that highly effective teams were frequently characterised by the following hierarchy. The foundation was a high level of trust. That enabled effective conflict resolution. In turn, that enabled high levels of commitment to flourish. Finally, having clear accountabilities enabled a strong focus on results. When these five topics were not present, each absence was regarded as a key indicator of dysfunctionality.

Almost all the warning signs mentioned in this section are behavioural. The good news is that it should be within the power of any top team to fix them. The challenge is to recognise the signs, agree to address them and then to fix them in a sustainable way. One commentator on dysfunctional behaviour at work said 'fish rots from the head'. This is a rather graphic way of asserting that dysfunctional behaviour among senior people gets replicated further and further down the organisation. The implications for the tone from the top are clear. As some of the case studies have shown in Part II, problems at senior levels tend to influence successive levels of management below.

SITUATIONAL LEADERSHIP

Hersey and Blanchard's situational leadership model identified four leadership styles: delegating, supporting, coaching and directing. In the delegating style, the leader displays low supportive and low directive behaviour. The emphasis is on responsibility and accountability within known guidelines. In the supportive style, leaders display high supportive and low directive behaviour. The emphasis is on high support within the autonomy given. In the coaching style, the leader displays high directive and high supportive behaviour. Here the emphasis is on close coaching on a short leash. Finally, in the directing style, leaders display high directive and low supportive behaviour. The emphasis is on command and control. These concepts are illustrated in Figure 6.

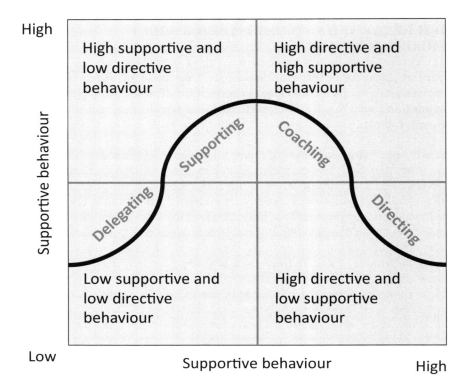

Figure 6   Situational leadership

The situational leadership model assumes that different situations call for different types of leadership behaviour. For example, where there are compelling reasons for change, one might expect a more directive style. Or as one executive once said: 'The last thing we need is a strategy, right now we just need to take out cost.' However, the unintended consequence of maintaining a directive style long after the crisis has gone is that, increasingly, people need to be told what to do. In the new regime, a more coaching style could be more appropriate. With stable and more benign economic conditions and with scope for more creativity, a more supportive or delegatory style may be more appropriate. Skilful leaders read the context and think ahead, adjusting their style as conditions evolve.

However, I would argue that promoting ethical business and an ethical workforce requires an unchanging commitment to ethical behaviour. The signalling that comes from this builds influence over the long term. It is a picture of predictability that causes people to stop and think about ethics, no matter what the situation or however benign or extreme the economic climate is.

CHALLENGE AND SUPPORT TO BUILD A HIGH PERFORMANCE TEAM

Figure 7 contains two aspects that are linked. The first charts the journey from a work group to a high-performance team. The second shows how the combination of challenge and support has fundamentally different influences on the work environment.

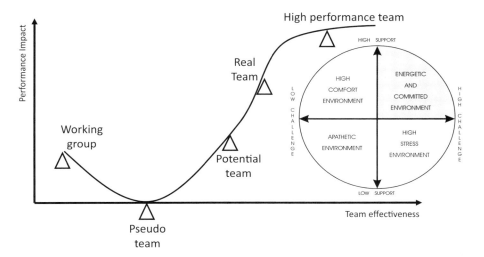

Figure 7   Challenge and support in building a high-performance team

From a Work Group to a High Performance Team

There can be some very effective working groups. The main characteristic is that they share a common leader but individual activities may be quite different. I have worked in a few teams where the diversity of responsibilities made team members think they had little if anything in common. Each person was self-motivated, needed little supervision and was very busy. They knew what they were doing and were getting on with it. But there lay the problem – there was hardly any team interaction, cohesion or any notion of the whole being greater than the sum of the parts.

A pseudo team is where people appear to get along well with each other and they are all very polite. Relationships are all very cordial and there appears to be harmony. The problem, however, is that there is little challenge and big issues go unaddressed. Team effectiveness is actually lower than that of a work group.

To use a well-known phrase: 'There is an elephant in the room but no one is talking about it.' This poses dangers because on the journey towards being a high-performance team, things often get worse before they get better.

A potential team is one where members are starting to have candid conversations and there is a willingness to listen to controversial points of view. In addition, there is support for and interest in other team members professionally if not quite personally. The good news is that in this model, a pseudo team has a performance impact slightly ahead of the work group. The journey is worth it thus far.

A real team is characterised by deeper interest in each other, both professionally and personally. It also includes mutual support and 'looking out' for each other. There are no longer topics or areas that are avoided. Issues and differences are surfaced, aired and resolved constructively. A dialogue of the deaf is not something one would ever expect in such a team. Performance impact is further enhanced and team identity is higher, more widely known and appreciated.

Finally, a high performance team is further along the curve, where sharing and offering advice and ideas enhances both individual and collective performance. By tapping into the diverse views and experience of team members, the whole becomes greater than the sum of the parts. High performing teams have high trust. A key characteristic comes from their leadership: typically there is strong evidence of high support and high challenge. The circular diagram in Figure 7 shows the various combinations of challenge and support as four segments.

Challenge and Support

Low challenge and low support creates an apathetic environment. The retention risk of team members is likely to be high, with few people staying long term. Also, the ethics risk may be high. For example, if a team member has bad intentions or is pressured or tempted to do unethical things, they may proceed if they think the leader is neither interested nor likely to find out. Low challenge and high support creates a high-comfort environment. In this situation, difficult issues are less likely to be confronted. There is a risk of 'groupthink' in which team members persuade themselves that their view is correct and there is no need to challenge, investigate or check. For example, if the team considers that everything is happening as normal, dissent or questions about the need to audit and review activities may go unanswered. This poses ethical risk. Often, frauds are committed in situations of complacency or where established procedures are believed to be foolproof such that no one looks. Bad apples can sometimes hide 'in full view' where the environment is too comfortable. High challenge and low support creates a high-stress environment. Here, the pressure is on and the absence of support also creates a retention risk. Such stressful environments are not happy places to be. They tend to make team members focus on ever-narrower aspects of their work, reacting to instructions rather than eliciting a broad contribution. The ethical risk element is that under stress, people might keep quiet about bad behaviour and ethical breaches. It is highly unlikely that a high-stress environment would encourage people to put themselves in the spotlight by raising concerns such as though whistleblowing.

Finally, there is the high challenge with high support situation. This creates an energetic and committed environment. Through this energy, a velocity of performance can develop. Also, levels of commitment are enhanced and frequently manifest themselves through greater discretionary extra effort. People 'go the extra mile' in energetic committed environments. The benefit for ethical risk management is that people are more likely to raise ethical concerns in such environments. They are more likely to talk about concerns, more likely to say what's on their mind and more likely to speak out about wrong-doing at every level. The work intensity can mean more people have more knowledge about what's going on rather than team members 'hunkering down' as so often happens in high-stress environments.

The balance between challenge and support and where a team is on the journey to becoming a high-performance team can have profound implications for the tone from the top. Senior teams collectively send high-volume signals by the way they work together. When a team is seen to be a team, one that enjoys an energetic, committed environment, its influence right down the organisation is beneficial in many ways. This can include a tone from the top that supports ethical behaviour and which facilitates the removal of 'bad apples' and the reduction of 'foolish' and 'tempted apples'.

LEADERSHIP THROUGH ENGAGEMENT

The Gallup organisation (www.gallup.com) is world famous for its opinion polling. It is also famous for its work on workplace effectiveness. In particular, over several decades, Gallup has undertaken tens of thousands of interviews with leaders, managers and employees across more than 140 countries. Gallup's work on employee engagement has used many hundreds of questions to elicit responses. What is unusual is that these have been distilled down to just 12, in order to measure engagement in a deeply meaningful way. In corporate life, many of us have had to endure employee surveys of 100, 200 or more questions. As leaders, we have also had to grapple with seemingly endless PowerPoint presentations covering the results from such data collection. The advantage of the Q12 is that it takes just a few minutes for everyone to complete and it applies to every job from the top to the bottom of the organisation, large or small. Similarly, results can be presented graphically on a single piece of paper.

There are two books that cover the research and academic rigour behind the Q12. *First Break All the Rules – What the World's Greatest Managers Do Differently* by Marcus Buckingham and Curt Coffman (Simon and Schuster, ISBN 978–0–684–85286–7). Secondly, and with a chapter on each of the Q12 statements: *12 – The Elements of Great Managing* by Rodd Wagner and James K Harter PhD (Gallup Press, ISBN 978–1–59562–998–2). These books cover the details of the questions and methodology.

Many regard the Gallup Q12 as an employee engagement survey. But that would miss the point. It is a powerful assessment tool of organisations' management and leadership capability. As such, it is also a powerful indicator of how the tone from the top translates into everyday actions. This is because where leadership has a clear, shared focus on *how* it manages, it creates a common style, a common culture. Almost all alternative employee surveys I have seen ultimately fail because results are gathered, presented and a report is written. Presentations are given and points noted. The presenter typically provides a list of things management needs to improve upon and everyone nods sagely, saying 'Yes, we'll get this fixed'. But of course, those things need fixing in other departments, never one's own. As a result, the improvement points are not properly addressed and employee scepticism turns to disappointment. Ultimately, many employee surveys fail in organisations where people rightly ask, 'Why should we complete this one when you have not acted on the last one?' Perhaps a common human foible is that, just as we like to think we are expert drivers, we all think we are great managers. In some organisations, managers also think they are experts at everyone else's senior job. The solution lies in holding managers to account individually for improvements.

To organise a Q12 wave requires a fully accurate picture of the organisation structure. Every respondent's answers remain confidential but are electronically linked to the manager of their section and the next higher manager. It does not compromise confidentiality because respondents are shown collectively in groups of five or more. If fewer than five people respond, they are grouped up to the next level. The survey is also heavily dependent on there being a full response from the survey population. In many organisations I have heard leaders boast of a 70 per cent return rate for an employee survey. That simply would not work with the Q12. It needs 100 per cent. An absolute commitment to leadership sponsorship and communication is essential. You may feel this is an impossible task, but I have run the Q12 across 33 international businesses, achieving 100 per cent returns in a third of them with very high 90s for most of the rest. The advantage of course is that this survey only takes a few minutes.

The questions are in fact a series of statements. Respondents are asked to score each statement on a 1 to 5 scale. 1 means 'I strongly disagree' and 5 means 'I strongly agree'. Many people think that a score of 3 or 4 must be a good result.

But to reach the upper quartile of the global database, scores well above 4.0 are often required.

Because the organisation structure is known, results can be presented at three levels:

1. The results for each manager, based on responses from people reporting directly to her or him. Five or more respondents enable the production of a personal scorecard for every single manager.
2. At the next level is the overall score for the function or region or business unit. In this way, a manager can compare her or his score to that of their overall function or unit.
3. At the third level, the results for the total organisation are given. Here, one can compare one's local result with that of the function or business unit and the whole organisation.

With graphic simplicity, scorecards show managers and leaders at all levels, how they compare to the wider picture. It also tells the organisation's top leadership who the great managers are and who are not. League tables of excellence can be drawn up and correlated against other organisational metrics. For example, by ranking the overall engagement score of each business unit and correlating that with business unit profitability, one can see how engagement correlates with the bottom line.

With every manager given a scorecard, the organisation can then start to set targets for future waves of the Q12. When I ran this programme, we said that the first wave would be for calibration purposes only. No matter what the results were, managers would be offered support, guidance, education, training and coaching. For the second wave, which in that organisation was run six months later, individual targets would be set. For example, if a manager's score from her or his staff on statement one was a score of 3.9, a target for statement one of 4.2 would be set for the second wave. If after the second wave, managers did not meet their targets, again they would be offered advice, guidance, education, training, support and coaching. And they would be set targets again for the third wave. Similarly, failing to reach target in the third wave would be met with encouragement, guidance, support, education, training and coaching. However, by this time it was increasingly clear who was pulling ahead versus who was lagging behind in their individual and wider scores. If after the fourth wave, managers still did not reach their targets – some of which were softened to help them 'get over the line' – everyone had to face the reality that those individuals simply weren't right for management. And they were managed out of the organisation. Some went of their own accord, realising that the climate and culture had changed. Some felt the pressure of the new regime. Instead of driving hard only for numerical results, the employer was, by now, just as concerned about the 'how' of performance as well as the 'what' of performance.

Across the world, great managers were identified and given a voice. Their achievements were celebrated and they were revered by senior leadership. High-scoring managers and high-scoring businesses began to have queues of people wanting to join them. Low-scoring managers had people wanting to leave. Leadership sent clear signals that the tone from the top meant a commitment to working with the methodology to improve engagement and drive performance, productivity and service.

So what was the outcome? Ranking each business by employee engagement score produced a list of 33 companies. Ranking each business by financial performance (using a suite of measures) also produced a list of 33 businesses. Lining them up was a revelation. They were the same list, line by line from top to bottom. Recognising that engagement is about commitment and discretionary extra effort, we calculated that the productivity increase grew to the equivalent of more than 700 people we had not needed to hire. Just as important, it became a better place to be and a better place to work. Almost everyone seemed to care more – about customers, about performance, about the business, about colleagues and about their own success. This was helped by the tone from the top. To an extent, it became the tone from the top. The CEO had run a similar programme previously so the path was easier having been trodden before. His sponsorship and unwavering support sent clear signals that the programme was here to stay.

Operational site visits took place across the world. The format was changed to start with discussions with the unit's highest-scoring managers: their best managers. Learning was captured and used to influence others, both in that business and in other businesses, sometimes on the other side of the world. The global network of conversations gathered pace as colleagues compared notes on how they were achieving great performance. What had previously been work groups became real teams. None of this was easy. It took huge commitment and was very time-consuming. But people realised that something new and different was happening. Managers now had to achieve three things, not just one: great financial performance, great people management and a great customer experience.

You might by now be wondering how a set of simple statements can be so powerful as to change the culture of an organisation and strengthen the tone from the top. Please refer to the books for the details. For now, I will cover the concepts in a generic way, but give you some detail on what happened in the company. Each of the 12 statements implies a flip-side that shows how achieving excellence requires concerted, unceasing effort. To read the full explanations, please read the book *12 – The Elements of Great Managing*. The following views are my own interpretations, based on my experience, which includes implementing the survey in a global organisation, with project management and process assistance provided by Gallup.

The first statement is about expectations. Respondents have to reply with a rating of 1 to 5 where 1 means 'I strongly disagree' through to 5 meaning 'I strongly agree'. The power of everyone strongly agreeing is that there is role clarity, goal clarity and managerial feedback to ensure people really do know what they need to do. Similarly, being clear shows there is at least some form of dialogue and performance management. The other side of the coin is to consider what leaders must do, to ensure everyone strongly agrees. Imagine a situation in which the average score is 4. That means people in the unit agree with the statement. However, it also shows there is a gap to be filled to get them all up to strong agreement. Some people simply are not clear; they don't quite know. And if there is just one such individual, they are not going to perform to their best at work. How could they? If you don't know where you are going, you will probably end up somewhere else. The opportunity therefore is for leadership and management to set a tone in which performance requirements are absolutely clear, for all. This mandates a systematic approach.

The implications for ethical leadership are now clear. By focusing on performance expectations, an organisation has the opportunity if not the obligation to explain the expected ethical standards to everyone. Adherence to rules, policies, audit and compliance can be spelled out and lived on a daily basis. Where there are special risks, for example of temptation, tighter performance and compliance standards can and should be clearly explained.

In one organisation, I ran a brainstorming session with a group attending a leadership development programme. The question was: 'What will we do for our people to deliver a score of 5 for the statement about expectations?' The response set out a blueprint for action: educating people on standard operating procedures, including compliance; a full set of job descriptions; proper, up-to-date organisation charts; proper, up-to-date employment contracts, including ethics compliance, confidentiality, protection of intellectual property and restrictive covenants; proper, written SMART (specific, measurable, achievable, realistic, time-bound) objectives; a mid-year and a full-year performance review; performance ratings that are explained to each employee. They added coaching from managers who don't just take an interest in what their people are doing but actively listen for signals, then feed back; they listed the use of Lean tools to improve performance and reduce waste; they mentioned education on the application of policies, environment, health and safety as well as wider aspects of the law: in short, they said that managers must explain their expectations so there are no doubts.

All of this prescribed a much more involved management methodology; one in which poor ethical practice or behaviour was much more likely to be found out. As we have seen earlier, where people think that the board, senior management or supervision are interested, knowledgeable and involved, they are more likely to find out what's going on one way or another. And that is a crucial part of mitigating ethical risk.

The second statement is about having tools appropriate for the assigned tasks. If there has been insufficient capital investment and the job cannot reasonably be done, it highlights the need for corrective action. Similarly, if equipment is defective, faulty or dangerous, this highlights any environment, health and safety issues that management need to correct. The statement also obliges management to explain to employees why things are what they are. For example, almost everyone in corporate life wants a faster computer with a bigger screen. While that might be a productivity aid, such over-provision comes at a cost. It is therefore up to the manager to explain why the current level of provision is good enough to do the job to the required standard. A further element of the statement reflects training. If an employee wrongly blames their poor performance on inadequate equipment while others are performing well, it is up to management to understand the issue, identify the training need and provide instruction or training to enable its correct use. The statement therefore requires several actions: provision of adequate kit, explaining why it is correct and ensuring employees have the capability to operate it correctly. There is little point upgrading a computer if the person only has the most basic office software skills. The requirement to explain and deal with issues obliges management to understand employees' individual needs and capabilities. Getting close to people and how they do their work enables management to understand their motivation, and potentially whether there are any situations that might lead to unethical behaviour. For example if an employee never takes any holiday, claiming they need to stay in the office to keep on top of backlogs, there might be something else going on. People who are reluctant for others to step in and do their work while they are away may have something to hide.

A leadership development brainstorm on this topic listed the following management actions necessary for people to agree strongly with the statement: appropriate software and systems, knowing who to talk to, assistance on how to do the job, use of Lean tools to understand and use the right materials and processes. In addition, they listed management explanations of why any computers and software are fit for purpose, the ability to raise issues or concerns, management taking feedback seriously, checks being undertaken, compliant work systems, safe systems of work and, finally, fit for purpose IT and telecom infrastructure.

The third statement uncovers how well people's talents and aspirations fit their job. At first sight, this suggests management should pay attention to job design and people selection. It goes much further than that, causing leaders to consider whether the organisation has the right fit of capabilities to job requirements. This places a spotlight on management who must ensure job holders are suited to the role from a technical, physical and temperamental point of view. It is also about enabling people to play to their strengths. Many would argue that once we get past our mid-20s, there is not much we can do to stop our weaknesses. Instead, success is much more predicated on our ability to play to our strengths. Statement three is all about that. Short-term training or job-specific training can ensure technical compliance, but a job that enables someone to do what they love doing and can excel at offers more. It provides a sense of innate satisfaction and vocation. In short, it becomes more than just a job. The challenge for management is therefore to find out what really fires people's enthusiasm and match that as closely as possible to the job and vice versa. If people are simply going through the motions, doing tasks that don't enable them to give of their best, maybe they aren't right for the job long term.

When brainstorming the third statement with leadership development delegates, they listed: adjusting jobs to employee strengths where appropriate, having the right objectives and the use of Lean tools to drive productivity and quality. They added regular recognition, support and supervision, management intervention to address areas of under-performance plus the removal of people whose job fit will always be a problem. Finally, they covered regular one-to-one meetings to understand where the talent lies and how it can best be applied, then management's understanding of employee successes, especially how and why they were successful.

The fourth statement is about recognition. It operates at many levels. First, it tests whether management offers any praise at all. After all, acknowledging good work is motivational. But the statement is highly time-bound, that is, specific. It obliges management to understand what work is being done, to know what is good and not good and to offer praise regularly. Such regular praise can only come from a good understanding of the quality of work done on a continuous basis. Secondly, it assumes that the employee has done good work that is praiseworthy. So what if the employee has not done good work? They would not be able to rate the statement with a '5' rating. That could mean there is a performance, capability or conduct problem. If there is and management cannot praise the employee, action is required to improve things until praise can begin again. Thirdly, an explicit timeframe obliges management not just to understand what's going on, but to confront under-performance quickly and effectively. The flip-side of the statement is whether management knows what work employees are doing, whether they know how good it is, whether they do indeed offer regular praise and if no praiseworthy work has been done, what action must management take?

Brainstorming the fourth statement with leadership development delegates listed the following actions: thanking employees for good work done and explaining why it is good, managers optimising work allocation to enable individuals doing great work to be identified and congratulated and the correct application of Lean tools to enable recognition of good work. They added management coaching, training or other interventions to assist the delivery of praiseworthy work and addressing situations where there is no opportunity to give praise. In addition, they listed management taking action regarding those who do not improve. They said that managers really must understand what is being achieved and not achieved in their departments. Finally, managers should understand how their people like to be recognised. As one put it: 'There is nothing more cringe-worthy than seeing someone put under a spotlight and made a fuss over, when all they wanted was a "thanks" in private.'

The fifth statement tests whether employees are understood as individuals rather than being seen as expendable resources. By understanding employees beyond the transactions of work, management can appreciate what drives people, what motivates them and what frustrates them. This more holistic picture enables higher levels of engagement. It also helps managers spot any signs of problems. For example, where a manager knows a trader is under huge pressure at home, has financial worries and is working on high-risk derivatives, it might just be prudent to ensure the compliance controls really are working properly. But if the manager has no idea about the pressures outside work faced by the trader, she or he could be blissfully unaware of the heightened risk. This statement is also about a sense of inclusion and belonging. Few people can survive in organisations where they don't have a sense of inclusion, a caring social network or an outlet for them to raise concerns outside work. In my experience, where people consider work to be a cold, task-only sort of place, the labour turnover tends to rise. If employees consider the culture to be a mercenary 'Just perform and we'll pay you', they are unlikely to associate with the brand, let alone the purpose of the organisation, its vision, mission and aims. This can be dangerous as it can spark unethical behaviour. If people feel no one cares about them, they might be tempted to ask why they should care about the employer. They might then take a more cavalier approach, turning a blind eye to malpractice.

Brainstorming the fifth statement with leadership development delegates listed: the need for managers to appreciate diversity and set a climate of team concern for individuals. They listed compassionate decisions, justice and fairness, decisions balanced on the facts and circumstances plus showing a mature interpretation of rules. They also mentioned managers demonstrating a clear concern for environment, health and safety. In addition, they highlighted that managers should show a concern for work/life balance and consider mental health issues, particularly in high-stress situations. Managers should protect employees from avoidable risks. They should know their people as individuals – their hopes, fears, pressure points and aspirations and also respect employees' privacy boundaries. Finally, they recommended that every manager should have a conversation with each employee once a year that has nothing to do with work.

The sixth statement is about performance improvement. At first sight, the statement tests whether management assesses performance at all. Assuming this happens, it requires an understanding of every employee's skills, capabilities and potential. The right kind of encouragement is important. There is clearly no point encouraging someone to aim for promotion to executive vice president of an investment bank when they haven't yet participated in a corporate transaction. Focusing on training and development signals a sense of career progress and growth. This appeals to basic principles enshrined in Maslow's hierarchy of needs. The personal connection is important as the statement mandates dialogue about performance, how to enhance performance and how to grow.

Brainstorming the sixth statement with leadership development delegates highlighted the following: managers should stretch and encourage their people. They should provide development in Lean tools and thinking and they should set SMART objectives. They should review employees' progress via performance reviews and development plans, and there should be a focus on performance improvement. In addition, they cited the need for managers to know what training and development is available within the organisation. They should provide coaching and feedback and encourage employees to 'own' their own development plans. Discussions about employee development should inform managers about employees' skills and capabilities to focus the right kind of support or guidance. It also helps to get job 'fit' right.

The seventh statement is about giving people a voice at work. People who rate this with a '5' feel they have a strong voice and are listened to. They feel a sense of dialogue on the issues that matter. Perhaps more importantly, they know they will get a response so they are prepared to offer their opinions in the first place. Skilled managers don't just listen, they seek input by asking all their employees. A participative style encourages joint problem-solving and a team approach to the issues of the day. It facilitates brainstorming and the use of Lean tools. Environments with high scores for this statement tend to have people who are willing to offer opinions – which will cover work improvements, elimination of waste, suggestions and how to serve customers better. In short, when people feel listened to they will be more forthcoming. Environments where people are willing to offer opinions tend to be sufficiently open that people will speak out when something is troubling them, when something is wrong and when they discover bad practice or bad intent. This can have profound implications for mitigating ethical risk. The obligation on management, however, is not just to listen but to act on opinions and feedback regarding what is accepted as helpful and why unhelpful opinions are not being taken forward. Communication is key. If the statement scores below '4', managers should think carefully about whether people would turn a blind eye if malpractice is discovered.

The eighth statement explores the sense of connection people have with the highest aims of the organisation. Most of us are familiar with the story in which President Kennedy asked a man sweeping the floor at NASA what he was doing. Back came the reply: 'I'm helping to put a man on the moon.' The cleaner felt a higher sense of purpose and was very much engaged with his work. This was presumably because management had explained to him that while his job might appear menial, it was vital to have spotless conditions in the lunar vehicle assembly area. It is up to management to explain to all employees how and why their job is important, why good performance really matters and what the consequences of poor performance are. Management must also understand and explain the overall purpose of the organisation. This goes beyond the brand or the employment brand. It goes to the core of why the organisation exists. Understanding this enhances commitment as people see the connection between their work and what the organisation is ultimately about. Where this statement elicits low scores, there is ample scope for misalignment, role confusion and conflicting priorities. Feeling a connection to the purpose of the organisation also connects to the values of the organisation. This can be extremely helpful to guide behaviour where there is ambiguity or no guidance. For example, if the purpose of a regulator is to protect the public from poor financial advice, an employee with a strong connection to that is likely to pay attention to clarity, certainty and follow-up when regulating external providers. They are more likely to understand why their work really is important.

The ninth statement is about the whole team delivering high standards of work. At first sight it suggests that management has a quality control responsibility. It goes further than that. It obliges management to understand each person's level of commitment to delivering real quality as well as the actual level delivered. Further, it obliges management to address under-performance. If the statement elicits a low score, that tells management that some people in a department, division, business unit or entire company are passengers. People aren't stupid, they know who the fakers are. They know who isn't pulling their weight and they know who doesn't care. The obligation is therefore on management to address the problem and to train, motivate, transfer or ultimately remove people who are not committed to delivering high standards of work. The key question is that if colleagues are not committed to high standards, what is being done about it? I believe a strongly positive score for this statement helps organisations and their leadership ensure compliance and correct behaviour. It helps organisations identify and deal with 'bad apples', 'foolish apples' and 'tempted apples'. As a tool for ethical risk mitigation, I think it engenders a sense of pride in quality and the rejection of sub-standard work, bad attitudes and, ultimately inappropriate people.

The tenth statement addresses social networks and the ability to confide in people at work. It is the statement that evokes the most comment and the strongest debate. Many people say it has no place in a work survey. Perhaps the best way of thinking about it is as follows: at work, is there someone you go to first for news, advice or other information? Is there someone you prefer to open up to – your first port of call? Is there one person who you talk to about hopes and fears, not just routine things? If so, then you would rate this statement a '5'. The statement is about close contact with someone regarding the important things that matter. It is one of the best predictors of labour turnover or staff churn. Where scores are low, people tend to feel detached or in extreme cases alienated from their work. They feel little sense of inclusion and are most likely to leave. No one is suggesting management sets up spurious social events or encourages forced friendship at work. But setting a psychological climate that does not hinder social networks can be highly beneficial. If people feel they can confide in a close colleague, the employer has an early warning system against ethical malpractice. Here's why: if fraud is discovered and someone can't even validate their shock and surprise with a trusted colleague, the employer stands to lose more than just money.

The eleventh statement obliges management to review performance. That in turn is predicated on proper objectives, which in turn is dependent on appropriate dialogue to set objectives that are specific, measurable, achievable, realistic and time-bound. Doing that is dependent on management understanding the skills and capabilities of the individual. The statement therefore requires a systematic approach to skills, capability, objectives, performance and development. It then requires management to use their interpersonal skills to discuss performance in a meaningful way that motivates people to aim higher. We have all seen and heard managers say to others 'Yes, you are doing just fine' as a means of avoiding a conversation on performance. But people need to know how they are doing in an objective, constructive way. I once overheard an employee tell his manager: 'Fine is OK for now, but we both know that tomorrow the bar will be raised and what was fine today won't be good enough tomorrow – so how can I get even better?' The manager realised it was time to level with the employee and talk about the things that mattered, rather than skating over the surface.

The final statement is about personal development. It obliges management to think beyond a transactional view of work. Even where people are good at a set of tasks, if they are repeatedly asked to perform them year after year, they will lose enthusiasm and engagement; eventually they will leave. The statement measures the extent to which managers are increasing the human capital of their workforce. By providing opportunities for growth, they sustain engagement through new challenges, broadening, job enrichment, job rotation, secondments, learning, teaching and many other aspects. It is a very short-sighted view that wants to keep good people doing exactly the same job – just because they are good at it. Too many managers stay as managers – rather than become leaders, because they are not thinking about long-term sustainability of the organisation. They should think of their department, division or business unit as an escalator in which people are growing and moving up to bigger jobs. As people move off the top (to promotions, other units or even outside the organisation), new people come in at a lower level and lower cost, thereby containing the total employment cost.

As you can see, the Q12 is not about 'being nice to people'. Far from it, it demands concerted action to manage and sustain performance every single day. The survey is not so much an employee attitude survey but a powerful tool to measure the quality and effectiveness of leadership and of management. It enables organisations to identify great managers and poor ones. Having done that, it enables organisations to set the right culture, a clear tone from the top and to remove those who simply aren't managing properly. Its real value is in enabling leaders to set a clear tone from the top that focuses on people doing the right thing, mitigating ethical risk, having the confidence to speak out and also confronting under-performance or malpractice. Where people care deeply about their organisation, I believe that ethical risk is likely to be significantly reduced.

THE BUSINESS LIFE CYCLE AND THE TONE FROM THE TOP

The tone from the top may differ depending on where an organisation is within its life cycle. However, fundamental ethics should continue unchanged. It is perhaps the emphasis that changes, allowing leadership to put an extra spotlight on key ethical principles as situations and conditions emerge and change. In matching strategy to the business situation, perhaps ethical emphasis should also be aligned. The advantage of emphasising different aspects is that it keeps ethics alive and on the agenda.

For start-up businesses, sales velocity, marketing, revenue growth, building customers and supply chain are front of mind. Basic infrastructure might be neglected as policy and process are invented as situations arise. The tone from the top will no doubt emphasise the speed required for growth. However, leaders should take steps early on to set the ethical compass of their start-up. Many start-ups fail for clear commercial reasons such as inadequate funding, an inability to turn prospects into sales, negative cash flow, delays in getting to market or competitors taking market share. Some fail due to unforeseen financial issues, people issues and poor risk management. For example the consequences of a bad senior hire early on in a company's development could be devastating.

For those companies that succeed, the emphasis changes to one of consolidating success. As companies mature, they build infrastructure and processes. The tone shifts to one of professionalism and doing the right thing as more people are aware of the organisation. While compliance is always important, its place on the agenda tends to rise.

Market change, technology change, people issues, a changing commercial environment and new competitors are just a few situations that may require organisational reorientation. This requires change management and clear signalling about how and why change is required. The tone here might emphasise justice and fairness in implementing change. Where such change is significant, such as redundancies or 'right-sizing', integrity and honest, open communication are essential to bring the trust of the organisation with you.

Rapid market change, technology change and sometimes people change can lead to crises requiring rapid intervention to recover performance. This can of course apply to start-ups too. Turnarounds are high-stress environments in which time is of the essence. Often we read in the press about mature companies reinventing themselves as 'the largest start-up around'. Mobilising a workforce to be committed and stay committed to a turnaround can be one of leadership's greatest challenges. Here, maintaining the tone from the top through process, actions, decisions, communication and signalling are of vital importance. Often, unforeseen problems are uncovered. The way these are tackled sends signals and guidance for employees at all levels. Crisis situations frequently include significant redundancies. The way these are handled sends signals to those going – and to the external employment market. Handling such redundancies also sends signals to those staying. Employees remaining will draw clear conclusions about the culture and ethics of an organisation as they observe what is happening to others. The tone from the top can be a great asset to foster team cohesion in the face of a crisis.

Many years ago, I worked for a one-hundred-million-pound turnover technology company that was eventually sold for just one pound. Its financial controller was a great leader whose behaviour sent strong signals regarding ethics, fairness and all the principles of great management. His staff saw all the red numbers, week after week. It was clear to them that the ship was going down. But no one left. Why? Because through his clear tone from the top, people trusted him and believed his guidance when he said: 'You may not like this experience and you may wonder how you could possibly benefit from it. However, wherever you are in your career, this is unique learning and it will strengthen your candidacy for bigger jobs elsewhere.' Upon completion of the takeover, displaced members of that function were among the first to get new jobs and the overall success rate was faster than expected. The proportion gaining bigger jobs was higher than expected.

TURNAROUNDS AND THE WILL TO RECOVER

Few organisations escape the need for significant structural change. Whether it is disruptive change, new competitors or technology, sooner or later a big restructuring is required. One leadership failing is a failure to recognise the need soon enough. When change is essential, it usually comes in haste. A typical approach is to agree wholesale budget reductions with 'fairness', meaning every department, function or business takes a similar 'hit'. Headcount is cut 20 per cent, 30 per cent or 40 per cent and some activities are sold, closed or outsourced. The focus is rarely on those unfortunate people leaving the organisation – quite the reverse, it is to get the casualties off the battlefield as fast as possible. But that sends a signal, which is noted by those who stay. It says 'You are expendable, a commodity and you are disposable'. People remaining often say 'That could have been me'. As the reduced departments regroup to work out how they can continue, there is a growing awareness of the loss of tacit knowledge, of process fragmentation, tribalism and attrition. One organisation that took out hundreds of middle managers in the imaging and reprographics industry realised that instead of senior management dealing directly with the shop floor, there was a communication breakdown and no one knew how to make the core processes work. Over many years, those middle managers had become the glue that understood all the short cuts, all the nuances and process work-arounds that enabled effective performance. Of course, things had become too complex but no one had driven any real process simplification in advance of the mass redundancies.

The unintended consequence of diving headlong into large redundancy programmes is often hectoring along the lines of 'Work harder, work smarter, give me more from less'. Sadly, most employees simply shrug their shoulders and ask 'How?'

I believe that effective leaders who set and uphold the tone from the top take action sooner to avoid knee-jerk cost reduction. However, where it is essential, the start point is to simplify the business model and take complexity out of the business processes. A new organisation can be designed by redesigning how customers are served, simplifying processes and forcing people to make trade-offs and hard choices. The signal this sends is to show that a smaller company will also be a more effective one. To be clear, cost reduction, cost variablisation, outsourcing, off-shoring and franchising may all take place. However it is in the context of the new organisation with its new business model, not the old organisation. Leadership's role is to reaffirm the values and show how change is being managed in accordance with them. A compelling new vision needs to be communicated through highly visible executives who demonstrably believe it. With clear vision, mission and goals, the new organisation can be populated fairly and those leaving can be managed out of the business. They should go with thanks and reward – they have undoubted skill and capability (otherwise they should have been fired long ago), but the needs of the organisation have changed. They should have absolute clarity on what the exit deal is and, naturally, compliance with all consultation requirements is essential. The way in which this is done also sends key signals.

One CEO I worked for stood up in front of the entire workforce of a large call centre being closed. He explained the service incentive plan through to closure. When challenged by a cynic, he replied: 'If this does not deliver to you the absolute maximum bonus, then I have failed.' Management supported the plan and performance improved every day right up to the closure. This underlined the importance of all managers being briefed, trained and highly skilled in managing through change, grasping the difficult issues and having the difficult conversations. Using data to show progress is really important. Not only does it keep everyone grounded in the progress of the turnaround but also it reinforces the pursuit of realistic goals. In turnarounds, executives often get accused of 'going invisible' – such is the number of additional meetings. They need to counter this with higher visibility, more town hall meetings, more audio and video conferences, more briefings and more simply 'walking the floor'. The message in the redesigned organisation, fairly populated, is one of 'Work smarter, deliver less from less', *but* deliver it more profitably. Sometimes executives lose sight of the benefit of having a smaller business that is more profitable rather than a larger one that may be less profitable.

With simpler processes and a new vision there should be a renewed emphasis on job design – what people are actually expected to do and achieve, and how they must cooperate to be successful. And there is one further element needed to give those who remain a reason to want to stay. This might be a new leadership development programme, investment in new products or services or the pursuit of new markets. However, something new and different is needed to demonstrate why the pain was necessary and how it is now delivering benefits. Without that, there is real risk of tribalism, disengagement and attrition of the very people needed for recovery.

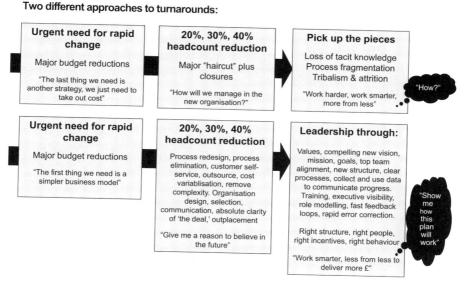

Two different approaches to turnarounds:

Figure 8   In turnaround, agility must not destroy the will to recover

THE WORLD HAS CHANGED

The world has changed and it has changed most for long-established organisations. For some, their tone from the top might have been one of consistent performance, following the rules and providing careers built on length of service. A kind of mutual trust based on certainty. Such organisations now must refocus on agility within a strong ethical framework.

Some organisations built an entitlement mentality: entitled to their market share, their customers, suppliers, profit margins, their jobs. That sort of culture is often one of protecting the *status quo*. The implicit thought is that the organisation has been around for many years and will continue for many years to come. However, when a disruptive change comes, such as a recession, the culture changes to one of protecting market share. As the disruption continues, sometimes leaders who may still be in the old mindset may think they can withstand the change. Such people are then walking backwards, slowly. But they are swimming against the tide. The question 'why aren't we winning?' raises its head. In this type of situation, the tone from the top needs to shift to match a realignment or crisis process: denial simply does not work. History is full of companies that failed in the face of clear evidence of disruptive change. Perhaps Kodak's denial of the speed of digital substitution was one of the causes of its downfall.

From recession and disruptive change comes the need for every member of the organisation to adopt an enterprise mentality. Here, the tone from the top stresses the need to compete for every cent or penny the company makes. The tone shifts the culture towards a more customer-centric one. There is a realisation that the customer defines the size, scope and scale of the enterprise. Or as one CEO put it to me: 'The customer is the only person who can fire the entire company from the chairman downwards, simply by taking their money elsewhere.' We live in not just a more uncertain world but also a more connected world. The speed of communication and use of multiple channels make an ethical tone from the top all the more important. In the enterprise mentality, there is a shift from back office to front office. Typically, headcount reduces in back office functions. IT automation and web enablement simplify and streamline business processes. Customer and employee self-service are now the norm. With a greater proportion of externally facing employees, the importance of a strong tone from the top has never been more important for building and sustaining organisations' reputations.

A pharmaceutical company was accused of unethical sales incentive practices. The story broke and social media were multiplying it around the world within minutes. As people added their own opinions, the story shifted and the company had little or no time to defend itself in the court of public opinion. Its activities were much more visible. The tone from the top was already emphasising the importance of ethics, honesty, compliance and obeying the law. But a small number of individuals had ignored that. In the crackdown that followed, numerous similar companies were investigated by the authorities and two of them were local to the country of origin. But the global story focused almost exclusively on the first organisation to be named. It was the biggest, the one whose global brand had the most to lose. Just as the authorities wanted to send a signal to other organisations and the wider world, the company needed to send clear signals that it was serious about ethics.

In the transition from entitlement mentality into disruptive change, leadership often implements incremental change, fixing the basics and having clearly defined end-points for each action. The danger is that the old mindset is still very much alive – both among leaders and employees. So it is rare that the tone from the top changes, even though it needs to. In the recovery phase and the transition from disruptive change to enterprise mentality, changes are still frequently implemented within known boundaries. There are, however, large opportunities for signalling a new world via the tone from the top. All too often, it is only when the enterprise mentality is achieved that full understanding of transformation takes place. Here, there is unceasing ambiguity with no end-point. Transformation is continuous and leaders have to assist businesses with individual issues while setting a new tone from the top, enhanced with a new focus on ethics, as the world increasingly looks on, passing judgement.

Leadership must implement change with integrity and a clear tone from the top

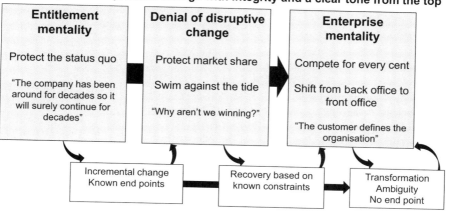

Figure 9   The world has changed

THE ROLE OF CHAIRMAN

In conversation with the chairman of a bank, he described his role and its limitations. He said there are really three things he can do as chairman: he can approve the budget, he can allocate capital and he can get serious about people. Beyond that, he felt he would be treading on the toes of the chief executive. This prompted a wider discussion on his phrase: 'Get serious about people.' This is best described as:

- Right people
- Right structure
- Right reward
- Right behaviour

Right people applies as much to board composition as the rest of the organisation. Particular attention was being paid to current and future skill needs of the board, together with the ethics of potential board members. While the tone from the top is owned and led by the chief executive, it was argued that the tone at the top, that is, the tone within the board, was the remit of the chairman.

Right structure also applies to the board and its committees as much as to the rest of the organisation. The chairman emphasised the importance of having the right board committees. In particular, the existence of an ethics committee sent clear signals about the tone from the top. The structure of operating companies and the type of top management structure were seen as important enablers of the governance processes. By keeping appropriate levels of diversity and balance within sound checks and balances of the power bases, he felt good governance could take place. The wrong structure could allow groupthink on the one hand or an autocracy based on too much power vested in one individual on the other hand.

Right reward also applies to all. For board members, reward needs to be sufficient to attract, motivate and retain the best, but not at any price. He spoke of the need for stretching performance conditions in variable pay for executives. He also stressed the need to listen to the views and concerns of shareholders. He was aware of a listed company where the chief executive had an unusual contract. Guarding against possible perceptions of reward for failure, the contract reduced the notice period by half for each successive profit warning within a specified time. For non-executive directors, fees should be sufficient, commensurate with the contribution and time devoted to the role. However, remuneration of non-executives should not be so large that they cannot walk away in the event of fundamental differences of opinion. He was arguing that independence could be compromised by reward so big that it suppresses rigorous, forthright debate.

Right behaviour was felt to be universal too. It is particularly important at the board, which sends so many signals from the way members behave both individually and collectively. The chairman regarded succession as 'the management of the disappointed'. That implied the need for exemplary behaviour from chairmen and women as well as those who are succession material, no matter what the outcome.

EXECUTIVE PRESENCE

Much has been written recently about the characteristics of leaders with executive presence and its impact on how they promote and extend the tone from the top. Executive presence is broadly defined as a constantly changing mix of three things:

- how one acts – gravitas
- how one speaks – communication, and
- how one looks – appearance

These three elements signal confidence, poise and authenticity in a way that commands attention, showing that an individual is worth following. They signal that the person is credible and should be heard. Much of the tone from the top at an individual level comes from behavioural signals that people pick up. We have seen earlier how many leaders are not fully aware of the size of the shadow they cast. Some are surprised at the extent to which their words are eagerly received, remembered and acted on for years. And this might be from a simple, short corridor conversation. It could be a fleeting moment for the senior person, but an audience with a revered man or woman for the recipient. Signalling from behaviour is therefore worthy of considered thought. Seeing ourselves as others see us helps all leaders set, uphold and maintain the tone from the top.

Psychologists use the Johari Window to explain this. Ingham and Luft developed this model for self-awareness, personal development and understanding relationships. Increasingly it is used to develop executive presence. It is helpful in understanding employer/employee relationships within the psychological contract. It is a disclosure and feedback model of self-awareness. The Johari Window has four regions – like four panes of glass in a traditional window. The first is the open area, the second the blind area, the third the hidden area and lastly the unknown area:

Open – what is known to me and to others;
Blind – what is unknown to me but known by others;
Hidden – what is known to me but not to others;
Unknown – what is unknown to me and unknown to others.

The standard presentation has all four windowpanes the same size. However, the panes can be changed in size to reflect the different proportions of each type of knowledge.

In the open area, there is information and understanding about behaviour, attitudes, values, feelings, emotions, experience, skills and opinions. These are known by the person and by others. This is the space where effective communication can take place. The second area is the blind spot where there is a lack of self-awareness. This can be reduced by the person learning from feedback. The blind area can also be referred to as ignorance about oneself and the impact one has on others. It can also refer to issues in which one is deluded. It can refer to issues where an individual is deliberately kept in the dark or excluded. People who are 'thick skinned' tend to have a large blind area. The third pane, the hidden self, represents information, feelings and views the person knows about themselves but which are not disclosed. The hidden area could include sensitivities, fears, hidden agendas, secrets and even manipulative intentions. However, typically, much hidden information is not very personal and can be moved into the open area. Self-disclosure can move information into the open area thereby enlarging it, to the benefit of others and the benefit of working relationships. Where combined with authenticity, this can enhance the ethical tone and signals sent. The final 'window pane' contains information unknown to the individual and others. It might include an ability that is underestimated or untried or an ability the person does not know they have. It could contain repressed or subconscious feelings, an aversion they don't know they have or even an unknown illness. Uncovering this information helps leaders to disclose more about their real self, aiding authenticity and enabling a stronger ethical tone.

CONCLUSIONS

In uncertain times, trust becomes even more important. The Edelman Trust Barometer reported in 2012 that the global financial crisis, resultant bank failures and government rescue plans had destabilised public confidence. This led to a breakdown in trust – of governments and business. High trust organisations find it much easier to implement change. Their people are more willing and more likely to believe that changes are ultimately in their best interests. Trust is a great enabler of cooperation, teamwork and efficiency. Trust increases employees' willingness to recommend their employer and decreases voluntary labour turnover. Conversely, low trust increases process times, increases bureaucracy and reduces visibility of what is really going on.

When corporate culture goes seriously wrong, often it is ethics and the mitigation of ethical risk that have fallen far short. In the summer of 2014, five former employees of *The News of The World* newspaper were found guilty of phone-hacking. In court, the employees' defence teams said that senior managers had 'condoned and encouraged' immoral and unethical behaviour. A private detective, hired by the newspaper admitted hacking voicemails, adding that his employer exerted 'relentless pressure' and 'constant demand for results'. A former news editor at *The Sunday Times* said that he dismissed a reporter for offering a financial bribe. This 'bad apple' reporter moved to another News International title where his 'exclusives' made front-page news. These examples show that the tone from the top has a profound impact on the conduct of organisations.

Part I of this book showed that it is vital boards set a clear tone from the top. Chairmen who participated in the original research recognised that ethical risk cannot be eliminated. It needs to be managed and mitigated on a continuous basis. They all recognised the need for assurance processes and for the board to send the right signals. Chairmen also acknowledged that they are all still learning. Most had examples of where their organisations had fallen short. A good tone starts with a good board. Strong, ethical chairs need to ensure there is a strong board with high ethical standards. As the case studies have shown, where executives respect and trust the board, the signals the board sends will have more traction further down the organisation. Similarly, if executives feel that their senior people, their directors and the board overall are interested and knowledgeable, they are likely to find out what is going on – one way or another. The expectation of pertinent questions sends clear signals that the board is concerned about issues and their resolution.

Strong governance is part of the tone from the top. This is far more than audit and reporting, controls and compliance. Governance as an ethos – which comes from the top and gives guidance to employees at all levels to do the right thing. One commentator said: 'great, ethical companies do the right thing even when they know no one is looking.'

While the tone at the top is very much the domain of the chairman or woman, the tone from the top must be led by the CEO. The board's role is to support the CEO. This can be done by devoting time to ethics, helping the CEO with difficult decisions and checking that the CEO is using all the tools at his or her disposal to communicate the importance of good ethics. The board can also make an assessment of the CEO's actual behaviour and the signals she or he sends.

The case studies in part two showed that the 'how' of dealing with ethical leadership is as important as the 'what' of dealing with it. Board strength is sustained through proper evaluation processes, combined with mapping talent to anticipated future need. This requires regular refreshment of the board, through planned rotation. Dysfunctional boards are toxic and whether they realise it or not, send dysfunctional signals down the organisation. On occasions, mediation may be necessary to enhance or restore effective working relationships. Such activity can be a model of ethical behaviour and an opportunity to send signals. Addressing employee concerns, whether perceived or real, is another way of demonstrating ethical leadership. By taking a fair and independent approach, with no pre-determined outcome, people are more likely to trust the decisions that follow. That said, once a decision is made, the tone from the top should signal appropriate follow through and implementation. Allowing constant reopening of decisions leads to paralysis. Leadership that reaffirms a decision to 'steady the horses' in the face of doubt can have a calming and re-energising effect.

Linking incentive plan membership (or any other form of activity that carries enhanced ethical risk) to the ethics code or code of conduct is a key action that sends many signals. At the very least, it reminds people of what the organisation expects. It removes any excuse of ignorance in the event of 'bad apples', 'foolish apples' or 'tempted apples' being found out. Focusing attention on ethical excellence and great managing also reinforces the tone from the top.

Consulting employees on major change issues in a transparent way with no 'spin' or agenda also shows an ethical stance. It demonstrates how leadership is committed to managing change professionally, ethically and appropriately. The tone from the top also colours behaviour and language further down the organisation. People tend to copy the behaviours and language of senior people. They want to get on. It is important that leaders act as role models and that they appreciate they are never off-duty, never 'off-stage'. Leaders who behave one way in public but another way in other situations run the risk of being viewed as unauthentic. The problem is that people do overhear meetings and catch glimpses of interactions. If the tone is not consistent, people will find out.

Removing 'bad apples' is necessary and it often reveals other problems previously unknown to the organisation's leadership. While the decision is rarely an issue, it is the investigation, the gathering and clarifying of the facts that can be a challenge. But the way in which leadership does this once again sends signals about ethics. 'Foolish apples' can be trained, educated and checks can be put in place to assure compliance. Where people are led on by others, tackling that head-on can act as a deterrent to others. Similarly, implementing auditable training while engendering competition through certificates and scoring can help to deter foolish actions. Clearly articulated values and training in the organisation's values can help employees think through the consequences of various courses of action. If nothing else, values guide decisions, actions and behaviour where there is ambiguity or no rules. Perhaps more importantly, a strong values-set helps others come forward and not turn a blind eye to malpractice.

Of course, politics and personal agendas can get in the way. But a strong governance framework with proper checks helps organisations to stay focused on facts and appropriate compliance.

Part III of this book addresses a range of topics on leadership. They are included to illustrate examples of how leadership practice can be used to create, reinforce, uphold and develop the tone from the top. A good tone starts with a good board. A good tone can only be multiplied throughout an organisation via effective leaders at lower levels. This section therefore addressed leadership development, giving examples of how various tools can be applied to enhance leadership capability.

Theory X, Theory Y, Action Centred Leadership, the changing requirements of leadership through a career and what is looked for in leaders, all aimed to remind us why an informed, holistic approach is required. An examination of leadership pitfalls explained how and why leaders can fail to make the right impact via the tone from the top. My own observation is that a task-focused approach often misses the point. As work intensity increases, perhaps we should say: 'Warning – high octane jobs can lead to tunnel vision.' A more '360-degree' approach, considering rational and emotional factors, usually leads to better understanding of what drives other peoples' decisions, actions and behaviour. No matter how good a policy might be, it won't be followed if stronger behavioural signals indicate it is unimportant. Barclays had world-class employment policies, ethics policies, codes of conduct and compliance processes. They had good people too. But the corporate culture, possibly influenced by the tone from the top did not prevent unethical LIBOR practices, which led to record fines from the regulator and changes to senior leadership. Perhaps every board evaluation should go beyond the guidance of the Financial Reporting Council and consider whether and how dysfunctional behaviours are impacting the tone from the top. The journey to a high performing team, especially a top team, is founded on high trust, high challenge and high support.

A significant exploration of the Gallup Q12 was included because it is a means of deploying ethical leadership across cultures and organisations globally. From personal experience, I can vouch for its transformational capabilities. Its most penetrating value is to identify who are great managers and who aren't. That enables leadership to demonstrate the tone from the top by taking action to highlight best practice and confront poor practice.

Different stages of the business life cycle may call for different leadership styles. The tone from the top may have different emphases, according to where any organisation is on its life cycle. However the ethical underpinning should not change. It is precisely because of unwavering commitment to ethics that the tone can adjust to different circumstances. For example, a commitment to ethical, fair recruitment is as important as a commitment to ethical, fair redundancies, even though the outcomes are poles apart.

I returned to the role of the chairman and the importance of this role in driving the right people, structure, reward and behaviour at the top of any organisation. While the chair is key to setting the tone at the top, it is the CEO who owns the tone from the top. The board must support and guide him or her in getting the tone down and through the organisation. All executives have a role to play and those with executive presence will be more effective, more influential and more respected.

Where organisations are considering a review of their code of conduct and perhaps getting employees, managers and leadership to sign it, a model code is provided in Appendix 3. Appendix 4 gives some insight into the topics that should be considered when planning an ethics audit – which could be conducted by an internal, highly respected individual or by an external person.

Finally, 'making waves' requires bravery. The tone from the top is a mechanism by which people at all levels can feel backed-up and given the confidence of their organisation. 'Making waves' has cost many analysts their job, which may explain why there are many more 'Buy' recommendations than 'Sell' recommendations. Organisations that enable people to speak up are more likely to mitigate ethical risk. I believe that a good, strong tone from the top facilitates behaviours that do just that – thereby enabling companies to succeed through challenging situations. And that is where behaviour might just trump strategy.

A MODEL CODE OF CONDUCT

Below is an example of a model code of conduct. To a great extent, any successful implementation will be determined by the way it is implemented, how people are trained on it and its meaning and how leaders 'live' it throughout the organisation. One thing is certain: if it simply remains a document in a policy folder, it will have no impact whatsoever.

When training executives on the code, special attention should be paid to the following 'dos' and 'don'ts':

- Do think about the impact of your behaviour
- Do consider the signal your actions send
- Do reflect on how you would feel if your actions were reported in the press
- Do consider how other parties would react to your decisions
- Do uphold exemplary interpersonal behaviour
- Do treat people in a fair, courteous and respectful manner
- Do disclose anything you are unsure about
- Do seek approval for gifts and disclose them

- Don't act without thinking
- Don't ignore contraventions of the Code
- Don't try to hide inappropriate behaviour or actions
- Don't treat people with disrespect
- Don't accept or give gifts that could be regarded as a bribe
- Don't assume someone else will fix a problem

The code can be used to promote the tone from the top in many different types of organisation. Demonstrating senior executive commitment to it and sending signals through 'consequence management' (that is, there are clear consequences for those who do not comply with or uphold the code) illustrate and emphasise the tone.

CODE OF CONDUCT

Our success relies on our commitment to sound business conduct and how we interact with our shareholders, employees, customers, business partners and suppliers, communities, society and the environment. Our code of conduct applies to all our companies, to our employees and contractors. Where we operate with business partners, third parties or in joint venture arrangements where we do not have management control, we aim to promote the full application of the code of conduct.

STANDARDS OF BEHAVIOUR

We conduct our operations with honesty, integrity and openness. We respect the human rights and interests of our people. We respect the legitimate interests of all those with whom we have relationships.

OBEYING THE LAW

Our companies and our employees must comply with the laws and regulations of the countries where we operate.

SHAREHOLDERS

We will conduct our operations according to accepted principles of good corporate governance.

EMPLOYEES

We are committed to providing a working environment where employees can realise their full potential and contribute to business success. We respect the dignity of the individual. We support the Universal Declaration of Human Rights and the International Labour Organisation Core Conventions. We are committed to diversity in a working environment where there is mutual trust and respect and where everyone is accountable for their actions. We want everyone to feel responsible for the performance and reputation of our company. We aim to recruit, employ and promote employees only on the basis of their ability to meet the requirements of the job. We are committed to developing and enhancing each employee's skills and capabilities. We will provide our employees with safe and healthy working conditions and practices. We monitor and report our health and safety performance.

CUSTOMERS

We are committed to providing high-quality, good-value products and services that meet all applicable safety standards. We value the trust our customers place in us and will safeguard the information provided to us according to relevant laws and contractual commitments.

BUSINESS PARTNERS AND SUPPLIERS

We are committed to establishing mutually beneficial relations with our suppliers, customers and business partners. We will protect our property (including intellectual property) and respect the property of others. In our business dealings we expect our partners to respect our business principles.

COMMUNICATIONS

We will communicate openly within the bounds of commercial confidentiality and the law. We will ensure that all announcements are accurate, fair, timely and understandable, taking into account applicable standards.

BUSINESS INTEGRITY

We will not give or receive, directly or indirectly, bribes or other improper advantages for business or financial gain. No employee may offer, give or receive any gift or payment which is, or may reasonably be construed as being, a bribe. All gifts to employees over a minimum value will be disclosed and recorded.

CONFLICTS OF INTERESTS

All our people must avoid personal activities and financial interests that could conflict, or be perceived to conflict, with their responsibilities to the company. Our employees must not seek gain for themselves or others through misuse of their positions. Any circumstances that could give rise to a potential conflict of interest must be fully disclosed to the company and recorded.

COMPETITION

We are committed to operating vigorously yet fairly. We will conduct our operations according to the principles of fair competition.

COMMUNITY INVOLVEMENT

We acknowledge the interdependency between our business success and the wellbeing of the communities where we operate. We are committed to making a positive social contribution within those communities and acknowledge our responsibility to engage with the communities where we work.

THE ENVIRONMENT

We are committed to making continuous improvements in the management of our environmental impact as part of our goal of developing a sustainable business. We work to promote environmental care and awareness with emphasis on the need to reduce energy consumption and waste production. We monitor and report on environmental management.

COMPLIANCE – MONITORING – REPORTING

Compliance with this code of conduct is essential to our business success. The board is responsible for ensuring this code of conduct is communicated, understood and observed by all employees. Day-to-day responsibility for promoting and implementing the code is delegated to the senior management of each operating company. Compliance with the code is subject to review by the board through the audit committee. The board requires employees to bring to its attention, or to that of senior management, any breach or suspected breach of the code. We have whistleblowing procedures which allow employees to report breaches confidentially and anonymously.

GIFT POLICY

Offers of gifts (including corporate hospitality) from current or potential suppliers are part of day-to-day working life for certain employees. It is important, however, that any gift that might be perceived as materially influencing an employee's relationship with the donor (and which could therefore be perceived as a bribe) should not be accepted. As a guide, significant gifts and hospitality that you believe might have a value in excess of £XXX should only be accepted with prior approval from your line manager. However, if you feel that your acceptance of any lesser-valued gift might be perceived as an influence on your future actions, you should consider whether or not to accept it and, if you do accept it, you should disclose it.

Employee declaration: please fill in and return a pdf or scanned copy of this final page by email to

[NAME] Director [email address]

Name:_____Job title_____

Business unit_____My manager's name_____

I confirm that I have read and understood this Code of Conduct and Gift Policy and I commit to upholding and enforcing them within my organisation. I also understand that failure to comply with the code and gift policy may result in disciplinary action including dismissal. Further, I am aware that in serious cases it may also lead to criminal charges.

Signed_____Date_____

AN ETHICS AUDIT

AUDITING THE ETHICS OF THE ORGANISATION

The following check list outlines areas for action and review that should be considered when planning an ethics audit.

The board – the chair sets a clear tone at the top for the board to act as ethical role models. The CEO visibly owns the tone from the top and develops it through the organisation. The board manages ethical risk via an array of different channels including governance, processes, signals, behaviour and the way decisions are made known. The values of the organisation are lived by all board members. The board makes examples of serious non-compliance and shows impartiality, justice and fairness. There is a board committee that considers ethical matters. The board is given training on ethical matters and uses this to send signals to all employees. The tone from the top sets clear expectations of what should be on the agenda of all management meetings, for example environment, health, safety, whistleblowing and ethical matters. Ethical breach reports are reviewed by the board, which can compare and contrast the different parts of the business. Decisions and communications around ethical breaches are clear and pervasive. Symbolic actions are taken by the board. Rewards and incentives do not lead to ethical risk because of excessive temptation.

Management – managers act on clear guidance from the top and are well trained and well versed in the ethics policies, how to use them to best effect and how to make them 'live'. There is no victimisation or discrimination against whistle blowers. Management know, understand and live the values of the organisation. Management makes examples of serious non-compliance and shows impartiality, justice and fairness. There is open communication about ethical matters. Communications regarding who is hired, promoted and fired are clear and address ethical matters rather than obscure them. Symbolic actions are taken by management. Rewards and incentives do not lead to ethical risk because of excessive temptation. Special management attention is given to areas of heightened ethical risk. All managers are well versed in the different nature of ethical risk linked to 'bad apples', 'foolish apples' and 'tempted apples'.

All employees – employees are given appropriate, timely training on ethical matters. Employees give high marks for ethical matters in the employee survey. There is no fear culture. Employees feel encouraged to speak up and speak out against poor ethics. There is a culture of mitigating ethical risk based on openness. Employees are guided by the organisation's values in situations where there is little guidance or there is ambiguity. There is open communication about ethical matters and trust in the system. Employees will ask for help where they need guidance on ethical matters. Employees know why people leave the organisation when there are ethical breaches and trust the organisation to demonstrate impartiality, justice and fairness. Ethical risks are managed down a reducing curve of incidence and seriousness. Rewards and incentives do not lead to ethical risk because of excessive temptation.

INPUT MEASURES

Values – not only does the organisation have a published set of values but also all employees have them, know them and abide by them. Corrective action is taken against non-compliance. All new employees are trained in the values.

Code of conduct – not only does the organisation have a code of conduct but all employees are required to sign it. Those working in areas of high ethical risk may have additional elements in the code applicable to them. Audit and control are strengthened in such areas.

Training in the values – training takes place at regular intervals and is for all employees at all levels.

Measurement of the effectiveness of that training – feedback loops exist to test the effectiveness of training in the values.

Frequency of training in ethical matters – this is tracked and the timing is considered at board level, based on the need both for regular updates and driven by events. Signalling is maximised when events require update training.

Appraisals include an evaluation of ethics and/or adherence to the company values – assessment processes for annual reviews, for hiring and for promotion include evaluations of ethics. This is not simply a 'black mark' for ethical lapses but a rating for how sound the individual's ethics are. For example, recording how certain decisions were taken and enacted.

Whistleblowing – the policy exists, details are clearly available to all employees at all levels. Training is in place for new employees and all via a refreshment training plan. When asked 'If something was really troubling you at work, what would you do?' all employees can give a satisfactory answer and know who to contact, how to contact them and how to raise an issue. Employees at all levels using the whistleblowing policy are not victimised or discriminated against. There is trust in the system. Board level reviews of whistleblowing issues cover matters of substance, not trivia.

Exit interviews – a policy exists and documented interviews take place. Information is collected in reportable formats than can be grouped and consolidated. Learning is fed back in ways that do not prejudice the disclosure of information. Sometimes using external interviewers may help. Also, conducting exit interviews several months after someone has left may elicit more information after the initial emotion has passed.

The employee survey includes questions on ethics and values – these are tracked and reported to senior management and the board. Managers of departments with high and low scores are noted by the board.

Reputation evaluation – the organisation monitors its reputation on the web, in social media, in blogs as well as in the press and traditional media. Monitoring comments and criticism can help identify whether the views expressed indicate an inadequate ethical culture.

The tone of management communications – organisations should check for consistency between communications in emails, on noticeboards and intranets with the tone of leadership's speaking and behaviour.

OUTPUT MEASURES

Outcomes from employee surveys inform board action – such information is given proper consideration by the board.

Managers are given individual targets from employee surveys – based on understanding who presides over a department or function with high and low scores on ethical matters, individual targets can be set and monitored.

Managers with less than perfect ratings on ethics and values are tracked – a log is kept and, where necessary, additional controls established. Limits of authority and/ or powers of discretion may be curtailed.

The number of ethical incidents is tracked – by total company, by business unit, by division, by function and by department. The number is monitored by the board.

The locations/businesses/countries with ethical incidents are tracked – to enable regional comparisons and to identify those parts of the business whose results appear too good to be true.

Results from ethical audits are reviewed by the board and reported – they are reported back to the business and to external stakeholders, including via the annual report and accounts.

The amount and value of business turned away due to ethical concerns is tracked – such information is segmented to show 'hot spots' by volume and value. Special training can be put in place to mitigate ethical risk in areas of business type, business value, business location and competitive intensity. Communication mechanisms are in place to inform all employees of business turned away and why to extend learning.

Customer complaints – these are tracked and correlated with other measures such as labour turnover, employee relations problems, absence and management issues. If for example a pattern emerges of inadequate responses to customer grievances, it could indicate a poor tone from the top. It could even indicate conditions enabling fraud to go undetected.

A systematic approach to setting the tone from the top, including a clear strategy for managing ethical risk, should significantly reduce risk from 'bad apples', 'foolish apples' and 'tempted apples'. That approach should include the use of both input measures – what is being done to ensure ethical behaviour – and output measures – are all members of the company behaving ethically?

Designing and running an ethics audit consumes a considerable amount of manpower and time. It also produces a large quantity of data to be segmented, analysed and consolidated. Boards should think carefully about how such data is presented and then communicated to achieve maximum learning and secure a commitment to action and improvement. In a busy world with short attention spans, it is all too easy to ignore this vital subject. However, conducting an ethics audit could pave the way to mitigating untold risk. And that ultimately could sustain the very existence of the organisation.

MEETING BEHAVIOUR

MEETING BEHAVIOUR AS A MEANS OF SIGNALLING THE TONE FROM THE TOP

Finally, this appendix covers some aspects of ethical behaviour in meetings because leadership can use them every day of the week.

Leaders demonstrate the tone from the top at every interaction they have. Meetings in particular are an opportunity to display executive presence and high ethics. The following pointers have been found useful by countless managers and leaders:

START ON TIME

- Keep to the agenda
- Stick to the point
- No private meetings
- No interruptions or walk-outs
- Are you being constructive?
- Are you listening?
- Agree conclusions and actions

FINISH ON TIME

Things that can seriously damage your meetings:

- Justify
- Agree/disagree
- Find the flaw
- Jump in at the pause
- Answer not remotely close to the question

The word 'justify' is used to show that if people in meetings constantly have to justify what they say, there is a lack of trust. There is little point in persisting or repeating the point until the trust problem is fixed. As a result, anyone wanting to demonstrate high ethics via their own tone from the top should be on the lookout for this. Fixing trust is key to removing the need for justification. 'Agree/ disagree' refers to the ping-pong of claim and counter-claim. Unchecked, this can degenerate into a comical dialogue of the deaf. 'Find the flaw' refers to the blind spot that cannot see opportunity, only what is wrong with a statement, view or position. Jumping in at the pause refers to the annoying habit some people have of interrupting those who are struggling with a complex idea. Sometimes thinking aloud can bring great sparks of insight. But they will be damped down or prevented by interruptions. The tone should therefore enable people to have their say, even if sometimes they have to struggle with the words. Finally, 'Answer not remotely close to the question' is self-explanatory. This annoying trait is a warning sign of political behaviour, a lack of openness or a lack of trust. It can also indicate that people are not listening – instead choosing to go on a campaign about some pet project or idea. In all these cases, the tone from the top should exert a measure of control to bring out all contributions and then to decisions that are understood and supported.

In my non-executive role at a regulatory organisation, I am involved with the chairs of board committees and in their selection. As you might expect, selection criteria include confidence, competence and commitment. Additional elements we look for are the ability to elicit contributions from all at the meeting, to balance the various personalities and to bring points to a decision that is understood by all. As far as reasonably possible, we look for evidence of building consensus such that where someone's contribution is not taken forward, or their opinion is not accepted, they consider it to have been handled appropriately.

In board evaluations, typical questions regarding the Chair include the following:

- The Chair demonstrates effective leadership of the board
- The Chair's leadership style promotes constructive debate yet ensures the board works as a team
- The Chair enables the board to reach clear decisions which are understood by all members of the board

These questions provide guidance on how leadership should contribute to effective meetings. Through a combination of setting the tone, their executive presence and process skill, leaders can enhance meeting effectiveness.

INDEX

values (most frequent mentions), 11, 17,
    23, 30, 41, 71, 80, 119, 128
Videotron, 72
Virgin Media, 72

whistleblowing, 11, 16, 17, 18, 20, 21,
    24–7, 32, 35, 36, 41, 43, 128
William Hill plc, 8

Wincanton plc, 8
Wolseley plc, 8
working capital, 49, 55–6

Yorkshire Building Society, The, 1

Zurich Insurance, 6

If you have found this book useful you may be interested in other titles from Gower

Collaborative Wisdom
From Pervasive Logic to Effective Operational Leadership
Greg Park
9781409434603 (hardback)
9781409434610 (e-book – PDF)
9781409473541 (e-book – ePUB)

New Normal, Radical Shift
Changing Business and Politics for a Sustainable Future
Neela Bettridge and Philip Whiteley
9781409455745 (hardback)
9781409455752 (e-book – PDF)
9781472408198 (e-book – ePUB)

Corporate Community Involvement
A Visible Face of CSR in Practice
Bilge Uyan-Atay
9781472412447 (hardback)
9781472412454 (e-book – PDF)
9781472412461 (e-book – ePUB)

Building Anti-Fragile Organisations
Risk, Opportunity and Governance in a Turbulent World
Tony Bendell
9781472413888 (hardback)
9781472413895 (e-book – PDF)
9781472413901 (e-book – ePUB)

Corporate Strategy in the Age of Responsibility
Peter McManners
9781472423603 (hardback)
9781472423610 (e-book – PDF)
9781472423627 (e-book – ePUB)

The Open Organization
A New Era of Leadership and Organizational
Development
Philip A. Foster
9781472440112 (hardback)
9781472440129 (e-book – PDF)
9781472440136 (e-book – ePUB)

Green Outcomes in the Real World
Global Forces, Local Circumstances, and
Sustainable Solutions
Peter McManners
9780566091797 (hardback)
9780566091803 (e-book – PDF)
9781409459668 (e-book – ePUB)

22/9/16.